The Spingarn Brothers

THE SPINGARN BROTHERS

White Privilege, Jewish Heritage,
and the Struggle for Racial Equality

Katherine Reynolds Chaddock

Johns Hopkins University Press
Baltimore

Johns Hopkins University Press
2715 North Charles Street
Baltimore, Maryland 21218
www.press.jhu.edu

Library of Congress Cataloging-in-Publication Data is available.

ISBN 978-1-4214-4551-9 (hardcover)
ISBN: 978-1-4214-4552-6 (ebook)

LCCN: 2022008705

A catalog record for this book is available from the British Library.

Special discounts are available for bulk purchases of this book. For more information, please contact Special Sales at specialsales@jh.edu.

For Brett Reynolds and Adrienne Reynolds Cohen,
my greatest sources of professional encouragement
and personal joy

CONTENTS

EPILOGUE
Beyond Brotherhood 141

Brothers and Brotherhood

Spingarn High School in Washington, DC, was built in 1952 as a "colored school" in a "colored neighborhood" in recognition of the long-standing "separate but equal" legal doctrine. But it wasn't just another segregated school. Its imposing three-story redbrick building (225,000 square feet) graced a sprawling lawn and housed programs from home economics and woodworking to college preparatory academics. With fine architecture and interior amenities, as well as a legendary basketball program, it was one of the most impressive schools in the District of Columbia. Its gala opening event drew Black luminaries, such as Paul Robeson, W. E. B. Du Bois, and John Hope Franklin.

In an ironic twist, a racially segregated school—formally the Joel Elias Spingarn Senior High School—constituted the largest physical monument to a family name noted for efforts to end racial discrimination. It memorialized Joel Elias Spingarn (1875–1939) who, along with his brother, Arthur Barnett Spingarn (1878–1971), waged an ongoing struggle against racial separation in education, employment, residence, and all other areas limiting Black people's full participation in American life. The brothers were leaders in creating the National Association for the Advancement of Colored People (NAACP) and served consecutively as the association's presidents for a total of nearly 40 years. Two white, privileged, Jewish New Yorkers—one a professor, one a lawyer—committed most of their adult lives to the fight for justice and opportunity across color lines.

The remarkable school bearing the Spingarn name was only two years old when the US Supreme Court reversed school segregation in its landmark decision *Brown v. Board of Education* (1954). Although integrated educational alternatives slowly began to emerge, Spingarn High School, located in what

Spingarn High School, 2021. Courtesy of Brett C. Reynolds, photographer

was considered a Black neighborhood, thrived for several decades. Eventually, however, it succumbed to dwindling enrollment and graduation rates that sank to 50 percent. It closed in 2013. When a video team entered the abandoned building seven years later, footage surfaced on YouTube of graffiti-covered walls, peeling paint, discarded band uniforms, hungry rodents, and a basketball court floor buckling under several inches of water.[1] Later, District of Columbia leaders began plans to restore the building as a city bus barn. When that didn't happen, new proposals ranged from a charter school to a public school for professional training.

While a segregated school founded in the name of a white civil rights activist seems an anomaly, its gradual decline during the eventual spread of desegregated education can be viewed as not only inevitable but appropriate. It recalls the slow pace of steady, but still unfinished, progress in race relations that marked the dedicated work of the Spingarn brothers. A more lasting reminder of the family name is the NAACP Spingarn Medal, endowed by Joel in 1914 and awarded annually for outstanding achievement by an African American. Additionally, scholars of African American literary and artistic accomplishment can utilize the Moorland-Spingarn Research Center at Howard

University, which houses thousands of books and prints, along with archival materials, by and about African Americans. The collection was acquired from Arthur Spingarn in 1946.

☩

The paths taken by the Spingarn brothers diverged substantially from what might have been expected of the sons of Elias and Sarah Spingarn, unskilled workers and mid-nineteenth-century European Jewish immigrants. However, by the time of Joel's and Arthur's births, Elias Spingarn and Company (their father's wholesale tobacco business) was providing a comfortable life for the family. Their Midtown Manhattan residence, also home to younger brothers Harry and Sigmund, was convenient to the good private and public schools they attended prior to preparatory work at City College, degrees at Columbia University, and professional opportunities.

This dual biography explores the brothers' intertwined lives from their shared Jewish heritage and parental influence to their divergent professional directions. Their adult interests and work eventually converged around a commitment to racial justice, which may have reflected the combined impact of their family, their religious ancestry, and their financial stability. The brothers' efforts greatly shaped the early years of an ongoing struggle against bigotry and inequity toward Black citizens. They confronted both substantial difficulties and successes along the way.

There is no indication, in either their youth or their adulthood, that Arthur and Joel were much alike in personality or behavioral disposition. Arthur seemed more disciplined and goal directed. He began in adolescence to collect rare books and prints, which would someday increase in value. Joel, more unpredictable and adventurous, ran away from home at age 15 by walking to Philadelphia, where he stayed for several weeks before his frantic family located him. Both, however, quickly became avid readers and, while still in their teens, traveled to Europe with their father. From their mother, they developed a fondness for literature and art. From their father, they gained interests in foreign countries and foreign languages, as well as some knowledge of the New York business scene. Joel eventually would be described as appearing somewhat erudite and self-assured. Arthur typically was viewed as more approachable and down-to-earth. The brothers' academic pursuits also deviated substantially. Joel, the eldest of four surviving brothers, was expected by his family to experience immediate professional accomplishment, possibly as a lawyer. However, his interests lay elsewhere. He preferred a scholarly life in literature and poetry, while Arthur became the lawyer. They each met the turn of the twentieth century by launching successful early careers.

When Arthur graduated from Columbia University Law School, he immediately became a member of the American Bar Association and joined a Manhattan practice that specialized in corporate concerns. Joel, after receiving his doctorate in English and comparative literature, was named an assistant and then a tutor in Columbia's comparative literature program. He quickly became an author of widely published essays and verse and soon moved up the professorial ranks at Columbia. He married Amy Einstein, the daughter of a very wealthy woolen mill magnate. Their family would eventually include two sons and two daughters, who attended elite schools and enjoyed ample travel abroad. Arthur did not marry until age 39. He and his wife, Marion, a Manhattan social worker, had no children. Both brothers enjoyed the frequent international travel their (largely inherited) wealth readily allowed. Joel and his family regularly visited European capitals and US vacation sites, such as Martha's Vineyard and Palm Beach, Florida. Arthur's bibliophilic and other interests found him in Europe at least once or twice every year.

Although sharing little in their initial professional pursuits, both brothers were decidedly politically liberal. And, perhaps underscoring Joel's commitment to a life of practical experience as well as a life of the mind, he also participated in political activities. He joined Amy in the suffrage movement and many other causes. When they purchased a large country estate in Dutchess County, New York, they immediately became involved in local activist and benevolent groups. He was an avid supporter of President Theodore Roosevelt and easily gained the president's backing when he ran for the US Congress in 1908. Although unsuccessful, the experience added to his determination that a full life meant combining a literary life and a political life.

⚖

During the first decade of the twentieth century, race riots, lynchings, Jim Crow practices, and other racially charged events and issues were frequently in the news. In New York City, which experienced large Black migration from the South, the race question became particularly pertinent. In his early legal practice, Arthur Spingarn handled at least one civil rights case, and he was appalled at the injustice. He and Joel were equally shocked when they saw Black patrons at bars being overcharged and when they witnessed Black people being relegated to the back of theaters. Soon, they donated to the defense of a mistreated Black sharecropper in Arkansas. The case had been taken up by a collection of activists who were beginning to establish the fledgling NAACP. Within a few months, Joel and Arthur became involved in the organization's committees and meetings. By 1910, Joel was elected to the group's executive committee, and he immediately began tapping his brother for legal representation in suits against discriminatory treatment. By 1911, Arthur was named an NAACP vice president; he soon after became chair of the group's new legal committee.

The brothers' initial NAACP activities coincided—sometimes uncomfortably—with Arthur's growing law practice and participation in various civic groups and causes, as well as with Joel's recognition as a widely published scholar and his promotion to full professor. Any influence of their activism on their professional work lives—particularly regarding how they might be viewed by others—was complicated by widespread bias against Jews and immigrants. Joel, outspoken and impatient with university policies and decisions, clashed with Columbia president Nicholas Murray Butler on a variety of issues. When he widely shared his ongoing disgruntlement about decisions from the top, the board of trustees—a group of wealthy, white, Protestant businessmen—decided to discontinue his professorship. It is possible that his commitment to the struggle for racial equality, as well as his other liberal political activity, contributed to his removal from Columbia. Additionally, the loss of his position occurred at a time of increasing academic prejudice against the growing numbers of students and faculty who were not Christian and white. One observer later noted of Professor Spingarn, "It probably didn't help that he was Jewish."[2]

Like many of their Jewish contemporaries with roots in mid-nineteenth-century European migration, Joel and Arthur were part of a reformist movement, which enabled Jews to align more easily with Christian culture and to assimilate more smoothly into US society. The Spingarns did not live in strictly Jewish neighborhoods nor send the boys to Jewish primary schools. However, many scholars have noted a feeling of recognition among Jews who observed the plight of Black citizens from their own very long history of discrimination. Historian Cheryl Greenberg describes a bond based on a sense of "shared oppression."[3] Yet, David Levering Lewis adds, the experiences of Jewish and Black people were quite different—"intersecting, rather than parallel." He emphasizes that the two groups have shared "not a similar heritage, but an identical adversary—a species of white gentile." The result has been "a defensive alliance cemented more from the outside than from within."[4]

The leadership and philanthropy of well-known Jews in New York and elsewhere were particularly evident in the early days of the NAACP and the

National Urban League. In addition to the Spingarn brothers, these contributors included such prominent names as Rabbi Stephen Wise, Lillian Wald, Felix Adler, Edwin Seligman, Herbert Lehman, Jacob Schiff, and Louis Marshall. Urban Jewish liberals combined with New Englanders of abolitionist traditions to give prominence to early civil rights efforts. Not surprisingly, Arthur Spingarn was joined by numerous skilled Jewish lawyers in various court actions soon brought by the NAACP. As Ruth Bader Ginsburg reminded her audience in a 1995 address to the American Jewish Committee: "The demand for justice runs through the entirety of the Jewish tradition. Jews in large numbers became lawyers, some eventually became judges, and the best of those jurists used the law to secure justice for others." She then quoted former Supreme Court associate justice Arthur Goldberg's observation that "my concern for justice, for peace, for enlightenment, all stem from my heritage."[5]

There is no clear evidence that either Joel or Arthur examined their own motivations for their commitment to the cause of equal and just treatment across racial boundaries. However, what they sought was equity and fairness—concepts that Jewish communities could readily view as a matter of duty and obligation. Such concepts may not have been taught explicitly in the Spingarn home of reformist beliefs and limited religious discussion. Nor were they tenets encouraged in the secular schools the brothers attended. Yet, as members of a Jewish extended family, the brothers undoubtedly acquired views and ideas through example and experience. Further, although the Spingarns might not have encountered shared oppression or sensed equally demeaning treatment of Black and Jewish citizens, they certainly knew of bias against Jews, which might limit opportunities in certain businesses and associations. Thus, their religious heritage and contemporary understanding likely combined to underscore their commitment to racial justice.

After limited involvement in the earliest years of the NAACP, Joel became chair of the association's board of directors, then treasurer, and finally president (1930–1939). Arthur Spingarn served as chair of the association's legal committees for nearly 30 years before succeeding his brother as NAACP president (1940–1966). During their many years of leadership at the NAACP, Joel and Arthur faced significant challenges in shaping initiatives for racial justice that would work to the satisfaction of donors, members, colleagues, the Black community, and nationally elected officials. Arguments among the staff and throughout the membership were not uncommon in grappling with significant questions: Should the push for legal rights take precedence over the fight for economic advancement? Which legal cases make the best court challenges for equal rights issues? Why aren't more Black lawyers participating in NAACP court cases? If only segregated officer training is available in the US military, should Black men be encouraged to serve? How much and what type of support should be given to the growing labor movement? Arthur and Joel often found themselves smoothing ruffled feathers and justifying actions, to the alternating appreciation and dissatisfaction of longtime colleagues like W. E. B. Du Bois, James Weldon Johnson, Walter White, and Mary White Ovington. With their co-workers and others, the brothers could be generous and understanding. And they could be insistent and combative with approaches ranging from Arthur's stony determination to Joel's frank rebukes.

The brothers' aspirations concerning racial justice were not about an American melting pot or even economic equality, but about equal opportunity and the development of individual gifts and abilities. As political radicalism and socialist interests increased among twentieth-century liberals, that outlook could be challenged as limited, even patronizing, and without regard for real and immediate economic needs. It could also be viewed as reflective of the personal financial well-being the Spingarns enjoyed. Well into the Great Depression, with Joel as NAACP president, the Spingarns' commitment to betterment for the Black community remained the original aims of justice and equity. The idea of tackling economic issues with economic means held little interest for leaders who were now beginning to seem like the old guard. To many NAACP proponents, the earlier goals of achieving inclusion and justice for the oppressed now seemed too narrow for a Black community suffering in the 1930s. Debate grew as proposals for NAACP support of economic intervention divided members and leaders. It was, as B. Joyce Ross has described, a time of the "twilight of white liberalism" and the "eclipse of noneconomic liberalism."[6] Joel and Arthur Spingarn, with their decades of work for long-standing ideals of equality and fairness, were of an earlier generation.

⚖

Arthur's life outside his NAACP activities largely focused on his personal legal practice, from tax and estate work to literary and business contracts, and on his extensive book and print collecting. His thousands of collected items were largely works by Black artists, poets, novelists, and essayists, many very valuable and rare. He also became an expert on urban sexual health and morality issues, writing widely on the subject and often advising on related state legislation.

Joel's interests outside his NAACP work centered on his Dutchess County estate in Amenia, New York. There, he spent time with his wife and four children, became an expert botanist, continued his writing, and bought the weekly *Amenia Times*. He and Amy hosted several historic gatherings of racial justice advocates at their estate. He became close friends with frequent visitors Van Wyck Brooks and Lewis Mumford. After assisting in the founding of Harcourt, Brace, he spent several years as editor of that publisher's European Library. Both brothers enlisted in the military during World War I and served in France for a time.

After many years of precarious health, Joel limited his work as NAACP president largely to letters and occasional meetings during the 1930s. He had already presided over enormous NAACP growth in new branches, members, and donors. His frequent travel, speeches, and lobbying of federal officeholders had prompted public attention and political and legal action for issues from illegal discrimination to lynching. When Joel died of a brain tumor in 1939, Arthur was elected as the third president of the NAACP. Arthur also remained on the legal committee and was able to closely witness victories at the hands of expert lawyers Charles Hamilton Houston, William Hastie, Thurgood Marshall, and others. Perhaps most satisfying to him was the end of legally segregated public education with the 1954 Supreme Court decision in *Brown v. Board of Education*. However, by the time he resigned his NAACP presidency at age 87 in 1966, he had become increasingly aggravated with younger civil rights militants, whom he viewed as more concerned with Black power than racial equality and with Black nationalism than integration. He charged that their methods were "taking civil rights in the wrong way." Yet he also saw a somewhat natural progression: "We at the NAACP lit the torch, and they're carrying it now."[7]

The story of the work and impact of two vigorous advocates is also a story of disappointment and frustration with the limits of change. Federal law against racial segregation slowly advanced, while federal legislation against lynching failed. Racial discrimination in accommodations and elsewhere became illegal but remained not uncommon in practice. Working conditions and opportunities continued to demonstrate a divide between Black and white. While addressing these realities, Joel and Arthur could also celebrate the steady, but painfully slow, victories that kept the struggle alive until it was handed down to the next generation—and the next. Their story depicts the circumstances—personal and beyond—that shaped their ongoing commitment and their approaches to achieving lives of meaning for themselves and their fellow citizens.

CHAPTER ONE

Sons of Determination

Thirteen-year-old Elias Spingarn and his two older brothers left their native Austria in 1848 amid the turmoil of national revolution. (One brother's name was Samuel; the other's name is unknown.) Joel Spingarn later recounted with admiration that his father, Elias, had been "swept from his home as a mere boy by political and economic upheaval."[1] As Jews at a time when Austria was considered a Germanic state, the brothers also likely faced growing antisemitism throughout the region. They had heard of better opportunities in the United States, and their timing was excellent. New York City, which they would soon call home, was a place that could be very good to its mid-nineteenth-century immigrant residents. Enthusiasm for newcomers, new businesses, and new neighborhoods grew throughout the city.

As the Gilded Age approached, New Yorkers embraced an expansion of industrialization and innovation that spawned advances in manufacturing, mechanization, and trade. Mansions and skyscrapers grew apace with factories and railroads. In 1869, a golden spike hammered into a railway tie in Utah completed the expansive cross-country reach of the railroad to support continued growth. The Metropolitan Museum of Art opened the next year, followed in 1871 by New York's enormous Grand Central Depot. Immigrants who had arrived prior to the Civil War—first largely from Ireland and later from Germany and other European countries—were able to ride the wave of economic growth into the last several decades of the nineteenth century.

The Spingarn brothers had no problem initially finding unskilled work. Jobs were especially possible in the growing garment industry, where tailors and clothing manufacturers needed everyone from cloth cutters to delivery boys to shop cleaners. Woodworking artisans, grocers, and brewers also had expanding opportunities. Another industry, which was beginning to gravitate from the South to the North, caught Elias Spingarn's attention: tobacco. Leaves purchased in the United States and elsewhere could be imported and exported, bought and sold, and stripped and rolled into the finest cigars. About a dozen years after arriving in his new homeland, Elias established Elias Spingarn and Company, wholesale tobacco merchants engaged in purchasing, importing, packing, and exporting. His work eventually took him on frequent trips back to Europe, especially to Holland and England, as well as within the United States. With the growing popularity of cigarettes, his business continued to expand and thrive into the twentieth century.

Elias and his brothers were soon able to bring over a younger brother, whose name is unknown, from Austria and help him prepare for college and eventually graduate school at Harvard. Like many European Jewish immigrants of that time, the Spingarns' religious lineage surfaced as a reformist style of Judaism, with little religious practice of any kind. Historian Gerald Sorin notes that such Jewish immigrants typically aimed not at assimilation, but instead at acculturation. While sustaining their Jewish family and community, they integrated themselves into US society. The Jews of New York at midcentury tended to cluster in areas with German and Central European neighbors, but not necessarily with regard to any religious affiliation.[2]

In 1874, Elias married Sarah Barnett, 21 years old and a native of Hull, England, in the Yorkshire region. Also of Jewish heritage, she had migrated with her parents as an infant to New York City, where she grew up with two brothers and four sisters. Elias and Sarah's first son, Joel Elias, was born in 1875. Four more sons followed in quick succession: Harry (1876), Arthur (1878), Walter (1880, died in infancy), and Sigmund (1885). They settled into a Midtown home on East 58th Street not far from Park Avenue.

Elias and Sarah Spingarn were committed to providing their sons with diverse experiences and allowing a variety of interests. Rather than enrolling them in nearby Jewish day schools, they chose private and public grade schools for the boys—first the Julius Sachs Collegiate Institute and then a public grade school about eight blocks from their home. Joel and Arthur, however, later credited influences at home for the greater part of their early education. Joel, in a second-person biographical remembrance, called his mother's encouragement "profound," noting that "she sympathized with all his ambitions, and to her fondness of poetry may be due his own early literary tastes."[3] As an adult, he fondly remembered his boyhood love of Spenser's poem *The Faerie Queene* and its lasting influence on him: "I was profoundly thrilled by two beautiful stanzas in which the poet described the ideal of chivalric honor."[4] By the time Arthur Barnett Spingarn was 12 years old, he began using his interests in art and literature to invest in prints. New York art dealer Frederick Keppel let him pay 25 cents a week for a small James Whistler print. "I suppose he thought it was an amusing thing to do," Arthur later surmised. The thrill of the purchase, as well as his boyhood voracious reading, established his avocation of print and book collecting. "I was born interested in books," the lifelong bibliophile insisted.[5]

Elias Spingarn's influence on his sons often occurred through his business ventures. Joel recalled the travel that gave the brothers opportunities to "be in close touch with the American countryside from earliest childhood."[6] To Arthur, their father was an outspoken maverick and often entertaining—a "great storyteller" supplied with many humorous, and sometimes wise, adages. Although not politically active, Elias was a committed Democrat. He enjoyed recounting his attendance at Abraham Lincoln's famous Cooper Union speech in 1860 and being thoroughly unimpressed by the future president.[7]

⚖

The most memorable and stressful occurrence in the Spingarns' family life during the sons' early years was when Joel, just a few weeks after his 15th birthday, left home and went missing. As he later recounted it, the incident started when he and two friends planned a camping and trekking trip for a week or two in June. When both friends canceled, Joel decided he needed an adventure more than ever. "Something more than a mere walk through quiet lanes was needed to soothe my spirit," he later insisted. "I must have life, adventure, excitement."[8] Although his parents forbade him to leave, he managed to slip out with a knapsack and 60 cents. He decided to walk to Philadelphia, a journey that meant sleeping in barns and sometimes on home porches along the way. He ate when field hands offered him items from their lunch pails. When he reached Philadelphia, he began to call himself Juan de Lara, the name of a Cuban bandit he had invented for a short story he had written. After a day or two of paid errand running, he was lodging in a cheap hotel in a slum neighborhood. He was then hired by a story writer, George S. Richards, who was looking for a secretary. Richards, an alcoholic who was drunk much of the time, was supported by some wealthy relatives. He greatly exaggerated his wealth and abilities. Joel, posing as Juan de Lara, invented for himself a life as an orphan cheated out of an inheritance.

Joel's parents, frantic and with no idea of his whereabouts, hired a detective. A story appeared in the *New York Times* and the New York *Evening World*.[9] Posters were nailed on buildings and trees in various parts of New York and

New Jersey. Within two weeks of his departure, however, Joel wrote a buoyant letter to his father, addressing him as "My Dear Pop" and claiming he had forgotten to write during a time when he had "never had so much amusement in my life before." He explained that he was making good money as Richards's private secretary and was certain that "if I'd stay here another month I'd be a millionaire." He also included an address and cautioned his father to write any letters to his new name, Juan de Lara. In a postscript to his brothers Harry and Arthur, his hyperbole soared: "I had the damnest sport you ever saw in your whole lives. Assisted in writing a book; saved two men's lives; etc., etc."[10]

At the same time, Joel realized he was running out of clothes. His solution was "an affectionate, if rather casual, letter to my mother, merely saying that I had been having a wonderful time and asking her to send me some shirts and underwear." Elias Spingarn headed to Philadelphia immediately. After meeting Richards, who addressed him as "Mr. de Lara," Elias walked Joel outside. "I ought to give you a good whipping," he hissed. "But I think I will give you a good bath instead."[11]

Shortly after his return, Joel went to summer camp on Long Island. The camp rules and his penchant for breaking them, however, ended that adventure prematurely—by mutual consent of Joel and the camp administrator. But Joel's letter to his father from Philadelphia had contained at least one indication of his future intentions: "By the bye, did I pass the examination for the Freshman Class? Answer this immediately!"[12] Undoubtedly, his parents were happy that he would soon occupy himself with college studies.

⚖

The brothers' early schooling had groomed them for matriculation at the College of the City of New York (later City College of New York), which would fill in their preparatory work prior to university admission. Founded as the New York Free Academy in 1847, the country's first free public institution of higher education, the college enabled access solely based on academic merit. Its late nineteenth-century curriculum combined classical training in Latin and Greek and subjects such as geometry, chemistry, physics, and composition. The City College full course, combining some high school, preparatory school, and college academics, was a total of five years, although many students left earlier. Joel had begun his first year as a preparatory "sub-freshman" in 1889. The following year, after successfully passing his entrance examination and returning from Philadelphia, he became a true freshman. Although Arthur was three years younger, he was usually only a year or two behind Joel in school, an achievement he credited to their enjoyment of close interaction when reading together or coauthoring short stories. "We did the same things and read the same books, so I was ahead." He entered City College at age 13 in 1891.[13]

A more direct route to university admission—especially for aspirants to Columbia College (later Columbia University)—was Columbia Grammar School. It was typically accessed by sons of wealthy New York Protestants, a pipeline for well-bred adolescents who would become well-educated men of the world. However, with Joel's dramatic optimism and Arthur's measured determination, the leap to Columbia from another path seemed quite possible. Their four years at City College prepared them to enter Columbia College as juniors.

With resources that prompted Joel to define his family as "well to do, but not overly rich," there also was a great deal of education to be had through travel.[14] Their excursions began with trips accompanying their father to domestic tobacco-growing areas like Virginia and Kentucky. The summer of 1892 marked the Spingarn sons' first trip to Europe. The following summer, they were among 27 million visitors to the World's Columbian Exposition in Chicago. Located in downtown Jackson Park and on the Midway Plaisance on the South Side, the fair boasted more than 200 neoclassical buildings on 690 acres. It included dozens of exhibition buildings from US states and foreign nations, amusements and sideshows, life-size reproductions of Christopher Columbus's three ships, the world's first Ferris wheel, and more. The three eldest Spingarn brothers (Joel, Harry, and Arthur) traveled in August by steamboat and then train from Atlantic Highlands, a New Jersey oceanside summer locale for the family, to Chicago. They were joined on their 10-day adventure at the fair by an aunt and a 17-year-old female cousin.

Obedient to his mother's request for a letter every day, Joel described breathtaking fountains and lakes, model war vessels, bridges, gondolas, and aquariums. He was impressed by the "immense and numerous buildings—all white." The brothers particularly gravitated to foreign displays that found them walking through replicas of the streets of Cairo, the center of old Berlin, and the marketplace in a Turkish village. In the evenings, they were delighted with the beauty of the glittering light display at the electrical building. "There is a little too much to see," Joel reported. "One hardly knows what to look at first, what to see, what to avoid." And while the fair itself was a wonderful experience, he concluded that "the Chicago people are not very polite, courteous, liberal, peaceful, hospitable, or intelligent. . . . I should like to know if there is a polite person, a pretty girl, or a small foot in the whole place. The East is much nicer."[15]

Shortly after they arrived home from Chicago, Arthur returned to City College, which was in an impressive four-story Gothic Revival building at Lexington Avenue and 23rd Street. Joel had recently been admitted to Columbia College, and he began his junior year there in the fall of 1893. Arthur followed him two years later.

CHAPTER TWO

The Columbia Stamp

In the Spingarn family, the eldest son generally was expected to prepare for a career as a lawyer. When Joel decided that his literary interests pointed toward scholarship and teaching, it was up to Arthur to pursue legal studies.[1] Either son's route was well suited to undergraduate and graduate enrollment at Columbia College. Both Joel and Arthur arrived as juniors and completed two upper-class undergraduate years before advancing to graduate school. The campus they entered on 49th Street was a large cluster of aging buildings that included a president's house, chapel, library, classroom buildings, and some dormitory arrangements. Although outgrowing its space amid increasing student numbers, the site was comforting in its familiarity, and there were easy interactions among the students.

Arthur later recalled that when he had been at Columbia for a year, his father unexpectedly met the college's president, Seth Low, while in Europe. He introduced himself: "You don't know me, but I have two sons at Columbia." When he mentioned that his name was Spingarn, Low immediately exclaimed, "Oh, you mean Joel and Arthur."[2] Close quarters at the college facilitated student pranks, including one during compulsory chapel attendance, which resulted in a one-week suspension for 17-year-old Arthur. He and his friends sang the hymn "Nearer My God to Thee" as a loud chorus of "There are no flies on me."[3] Within a few years, however, that cozy and close fellowship of campus life changed. The Spingarn brothers pursued their graduate studies in a very different environment.

Throughout the summer of 1897, Columbia's faculty and administrators busily moved into new buildings in Morningside Heights on Manhattan's Upper West Side, a site previously occupied by the Bloomingdale Asylum for the Insane. The Spingarn brothers and their fellow students arrived in the fall to a sprawl of six new campus buildings alongside two still existing from the asylum. The change of atmosphere was somewhat daunting, but the college community was also giddy with anticipation. Frederick Keppel Jr., a student who later became dean of the undergraduate Columbia College, recalled "a sense of grandeur and confusion, . . . the smell of plaster and muddy footpaths, . . . magnificent but inconvenient distances between classrooms and memories of the crowded but convenient and familiar home we had left."[4] The move proved to be much more than a physical relocation. The newly renamed Columbia University soon expanded the array of its offerings and the purpose of its education to include undergraduate excellence and enhanced graduate and professional arenas. From 1890 to 1901, faculty numbers grew from 203 to 393, resident students from 1,758 to 4,440, and library holdings from 100,000 to 350,000 volumes.[5]

Eager to mark their new territory with new ideas, the students added a journal for verse and fiction named *Morningside*. It joined two student publications founded earlier: *Columbia Spectator* for news and *Literary Monthly* for essays. Joel Spingarn quickly became a *Morningside* contributor, as did other students on their way to making substantial marks in their fields. Those included Virginia Gildersleeve, later to be named dean of Barnard College; Hans Zinsser, an aspiring writer and medical doctor who eventually gained prominence for the development of a vaccine against typhus; John Erskine, soon to be a bestselling author, concert pianist, and first president of the Juilliard School of Music; and Melville Cane, who became a respected poet and legal counsel to numerous renowned authors of the twentieth century.

The pioneering spirit of settling on a new campus with generous space also prompted students and faculty to initiate new clubs, teams, courses, and programs. Student groups frequently presented plays and musical shows, and more than a dozen fraternities thrived on the Morningside campus. A sorority chapter opened at the women's college, Barnard, whose status also allowed the female students to access some of the curricular and extracurricular advantages of the all-male Columbia. Joel and Arthur Spingarn both joined the largest new Columbia club, King's Crown, founded by students and faculty a year after the move to Morningside. Its objective was "to promote sociability and to further a love of letters, but above all to afford [a] common meeting place for the discussion of undergraduate movements and the institution of collegiate reforms."[6] Encouraged largely by literature professor George Edward Woodberry, the group met twice monthly at the College Tavern; a formal lecture or discussion program at one meeting was followed by an informal social over beer and pretzels at the next. Regular student attendee Erskine later recalled: "How much of my education I owe to the Tavern! I grieved when it was torn down to make way for the Union Theological Seminary. . . . We learned then, if we had not already known before, how to be both cultured and comfortable."[7]

Professor Woodberry, a Harvard-educated literary scholar and poet, had arrived at Columbia in 1891 and quickly began to impress students in his literature classes. Arthur Spingarn later maintained that after attending primary schools and City College, "the first time any teacher had any real effect on me was in Columbia when I came into contact with Professor Woodberry, who had a very definite effect. . . . Almost all who came into contact with him developed a real feeling for literature." His brother Joel agreed, even though Woodberry was a dreamy idealist of the genteel tradition who shared little with Joel's growing desire to bring new and contemporary approaches to literary work. However, Woodberry's manner with students, rather than his literary opinions, earned Joel's admiration; he was "the greatest teacher our country has ever known."[8] Instead of lecturing, the professor held long Socratic dialogues with his students, involving them in speculating and questioning.

Woodberry's New England roots undoubtedly accounted for much of his impatience with realism and his devotion to a loving connection between life and art. He had studied under Henry Adams and Charles Eliot Norton, and he had attended Ralph Waldo Emerson's last lecture. This placed him in an old guard that, according to Joel, exhibited a "narrowness of sympathy which brushed aside the racier writers like Walt Whitman, [Henry David] Thoreau, Mark Twain, and Herman Melville." Yet Joel was impressed by Woodberry's deep sensitivity and patriotism. He also observed, "He attracted around him all the most alert elements in undergraduate life, athletes as well as scholars, and not only aroused in them a new interest in literature, but gave them a new point of view with which to interpret it."[9]

Joel's literary interests grew substantially as an undergraduate at Columbia, and he contributed poetic verses frequently to the campus literary monthly. His 1895 senior thesis, "A History of the Theory of Poetry in the Elizabethan Age," reflected his interest in probing poetic origins. Arthur's senior thesis, "Coleridge's Influence on English Thought," seemed less of a match for a rising law student.[10] While still teenagers and in a fit of scholarly self-confidence, the brothers had decided to edit the complete works of the highly prolific sixteenth-century British writer John Lyly. They eventually abandoned the idea of wading through hundreds of pages of poetry, drama, and essays. However, while at Columbia Joel got into a small skirmish with some British scholars when he wrote to an academic journal published in London and questioned their dating of one of Lyly's works. He was proud that his 1894 query in the *Athenaeum* was his first published work.[11]

☖☗

The Spingarn brothers enjoyed exceptionally good timing in their attendance at Columbia. They arrived at least a half dozen years before the institution's leadership began fretting about a "Jewish problem," which by 1919 would prompt restrictions on the number of Jewish students admitted. And they were able to participate in changes in American higher education that tilted away from the cozy prominence of small colleges dedicated to undergraduate liberal learning and toward new and meaningful graduate programs, professional fields, innovative research, and endowment growth. The Columbia name change from "college" to "university" indicated a readiness to excel in these areas, along with such institutions as Johns Hopkins, Cornell, the University of Chicago, Stanford, and Vanderbilt. Richard Hofstadter applauded the expansive and inclusive campuses of the late nineteenth century as "a system of genuine universities," which had been enabled when the "intellectual community began to detach itself from the leisured class."[12]

Columbia during this heady time adopted new fields in teaching and scholarship, including geology, biology, and psychology. In 1896, the widely regarded natural history scholar Franz Boas was appointed as Columbia's first professor of anthropology. In the same year, prominent musician Edward MacDowell brought his composition and concert piano expertise to campus as Columbia's first music professor. With the leadership of President Seth Low, who would soon become the mayor of New York City, undergraduate faculties were grouped into areas under deans for the first time. And perhaps more important, fundraising and civic involvement began in earnest.

Upon his graduation with honors, Joel opted to continue with his literary interests through graduate study, first during a postgraduate year in English and comparative literature at Harvard. Since he had never been far from home and family for an extended period of time, his experiences in Cambridge were bound to be both exciting and daunting. He spent his first week there searching for lodging, eventually renting a furnished bedroom, study, and bath suite not too far from campus. Next came registering for classes, purchasing books, joining a dining club, and writing home for various items, like a clock and a wastebasket. He was impressed with his new surroundings, writing to his mother that he was meeting "men from Maine, Illinois, California, New York, Massachusetts, and everywhere else. I hear that entrance examinations for Harvard are held in Europe and Japan. Just think of it! So many men! So many associations!"[13]

At Harvard, Spingarn was pleased to become acquainted with well-known and highly productive literary scholars, including George Lyman Kittredge, George Herbert Palmer, and Charles Eliot Norton. However, it was a visiting speaker on campus whom he later remembered as his greatest influence while in Cambridge. New York City police commissioner Theodore Roosevelt, reform-minded and politically astute, addressed a Harvard student audience about the complementary interests of politics and leadership. He admitted that politics as an interest or profession had a reputation of being "dirty." However, Spingarn recalled that Roosevelt viewed it as "the duty of you educated young men to get into politics and try to clean it up. After all, politics is the only way people decide how their society is going to be run at every level."[14] The young graduate student began to consider that political activity might be a calling that could happen in tandem with his commitment to literature and learning.

After his year at Harvard, perhaps testing the possibilities there, Joel returned to Columbia to work in earnest toward a PhD, the youngest doctoral student in his class. Undoubtedly, he felt at home with many familiar friends and students, as well as teachers like Woodberry, who became close mentors to graduate students undertaking individual scholarship. Graduate students in literary arts generally had smooth and highly productive interactions with faculty and their fellow students. Advanced classes, advising sessions with faculty, research, and writing marked Joel's graduate experience. An informal literary group on campus, the Society of Bards and Prophets, attracted Joel and others who wrote for Columbia publications and aspired to appear in journals beyond. John Erskine recalled: "We gathered in rathskellers or other places favorable to letters and to good fellowship. Fortified by a stein, a slice of rye bread with cheese on it and a dab of mustard, we listened to each other's compositions patiently, and read our own in retaliation."[15]

Predictably, not every graduate student of the time found the same academic stimulation in and out of class. Upton Sinclair, at the time already a dime novelist and a future political activist, socialist, and Pulitzer Prize winner, later claimed that while a graduate student at Columbia he found "the same dreary routine" he had experienced as an undergraduate at City College. Ludwig Lewisohn, eventually a renowned author and teacher, arrived after graduating with a bachelor of arts degree from the College of Charleston in his South Carolina hometown. He later claimed that he found the lectures at Columbia "dull and dispiriting" from professors who simply "ladled out information." He "passed creditable examinations without doing a page of the required reading; I had done it all."[16] Joel Spingarn, however, working with Woodberry's guidance on a dissertation on Renaissance literary criticism, was quickly becoming a young authority in his field. He often credited his mentor's "profound influence" for his academic success.[17]

Arthur Spingarn, selected to give the "class oration" speech at his 1897 Columbia graduation, made the first of a lifetime of regular trips to London shortly after. He then immediately moved on to Columbia Law School at its new location in Morningside Heights. Throughout the 1890s, the law school had undergone changes inspired by President Low's determination to position it to provide some of the best legal preparation in the nation. Previously, the school had been known for its relative ease of admission, which had led to high enrollments and revenues. By 1890, 60 percent of those attending the law school—which had graduated Theodore Roosevelt—were not college graduates. When Arthur Spingarn began his legal studies, the entrance requirements had become more rigorous, and a third year had been added to the previous two-year curriculum. New pedagogy included not only lectures on rules of law, but also Socratic approaches to addressing systemic and interpretive frameworks for tackling legal issues. Changes in the classroom also allowed for the use of the case method pioneered at Harvard. Columbia historian Robert McCaughey concludes that this more academically "elitist" conception of legal education "held that the study of the law under university auspices ought to reflect those auspices by the academic rigor—as opposed to simply professional utility—of the study."[18] That approach included a willingness to move the law school from its proximity to downtown courts and law offices to a place on the main campus.

ȡȡ

Graduate school in literature for Joel and in law for Arthur marked the first time the two brothers had involved themselves in very different directions, perhaps signaling their distinct young professional lives to come. During his studies, Joel worked closely with Woodberry and struggled to somehow smoothly meld theory and practice in his life and in his scholarship. He later explained that "poetry and philosophy and religion belong to the realm of theory. And I take politics as the highest form representative of the practical spirit."[19] He also became an enthusiast of the work and ideals of Italian philosopher Benedetto Croce, who managed to balance practical work in history and politics with a scholarly outlook emphasizing the spirit of the mind. Joel became familiar with Italian literature and philosophy, and his dissertation, completed and published in 1899 as *A History of Literary Criticism in the Renaissance,* became the first volume of the Columbia University Studies in Literature. It made a substantial splash for the youngest doctoral graduate that year. Biographer Joyce Ross notes that Joel's "simplicity of style, coupled with the mastery and critical discernment which he brought to his subject, won him international acclaim and established the volume as a classic in its field."[20]

When Joel received his PhD in the last year of the century, Arthur earned a master of arts degree that same year. He completed his Columbia law degree in 1900 and immediately joined the New York Bar Association.

CHAPTER THREE

No Simple Launch

The Spingarn brothers had always known they would not need to go far to begin their adult lives after Columbia University. New York City offered superb career opportunities, good professional contacts, convenient access to travel nearby and abroad, and ongoing interaction with friends and family. Their comfortable means and fine educations foretold highly promising futures. Their early career years also displayed a determination to encounter and accomplish at least some new and different experiences.

Arthur, who was uncertain about which area of legal specialization would be the best fit, initially tried several. He first joined the firm of Underwood, Van Vorst, Rosen and Hoyt, specializing in commercial issues. Although he found his colleagues congenial and was not unhappy with the work, he later reported that he "wasn't learning anything that was useful; I was learning how to reorganize railroads and things of that sort." With a goal of one day hanging out his own shingle, he decided that "although it was pleasant, I probably wouldn't have many railroads to reorganize in my private practice, and I left."[1] He eventually joined the firm of Studin and Sonnenberg and became close friends with Charles Studin, a Yale Law School graduate who shared Arthur's desire for more personal involvement with clients and their needs. Studin specialized in the legal representation of writers, artists, and musicians.

After the publication of his dissertation, Joel Spingarn was widely viewed as a young Columbia scholar of high promise. He immediately became the chief assistant to his mentor, George Edward Woodberry, chair of the Department of Comparative Literature. Joel was hired at the rank of tutor in the department and soon advanced to adjunct professor and full professor. During 1900, he traveled to Paris to a meeting of the International Congress of

Comparative History where he delivered an address in his excellent French: "American Scholarship: Les Belles Lettres et l'Erudition en Amerique du Point de Vue Academique." The following year, he was selected to read his lengthy romantic poem "The New Hesperides" at the Columbia Phi Beta Kappa Society, and he was named the university poet for the 1901 commencement exercises.[2]

Both brothers were interested in New York City social and civic activities. For Joel, however, that interest quickly embraced his penchant for close involvement, leading to what Ross identifies as his "unbelievable array of non-academic endeavors."[3] One of the earliest of these was his election in 1901 to the presidency of the Civic Club of New York City. A group of several hundred men, the club promoted reform politics and sought to curb the Tammany Hall machine by supporting local political candidates who would work for progressive change. The need to balance a love of scholarly inquiry with an affinity for meaningful action would be an ongoing theme of Joel Spingarn's life and work. He was intensely interested in public affairs at all levels and eager to personally participate. But he also found deep enjoyment in writing poetry and essays, analyzing literary scholarship, and sharing theoretical observations with students and colleagues. The first national publication of his poetry was a romantic verse, "Prothalamion," which appeared in the *Atlantic Monthly* in early 1902.

In an especially dramatic demonstration of his delight in action, Joel decided to spend the summer of 1902 conducting an on-site study of a continuing and very bloody Kentucky feud—something he might write about for magazine publication. The Hargis-Cockrill feud had started with a number of killings in 1901 in Jackson, Kentucky. Joel's investigation began in the nearby Appalachian town of Manchester, where he immediately met locals of all types, from feuders to farmers. He toured the county courthouse, which was pockmarked with bullet holes, and had no trouble locating Cockrill and Hargis family members. In frequent letters to Arthur, he recorded his observations in detail. Happy to shock his less adventurous brother, Joel wrote shortly after his arrival that "it feels funny to get shaved by a barber who killed three men in a fight." However, even though he could find "the rock bottom of human nature" among the Kentucky feuding families, he concluded that "many men seem splendid, generous, frank." He soon decided that the problem leading to the murders was twofold: "the universal carrying of weapons and the lack of what we would call fair play. It is always a fight for the drop here; a man's back is as vulnerable as his face." Yet he noted that various schools and clubs, as well as nearby Berea College, seemed to be working to make the area more "civilized."[4]

He moved to the tiny town of Jackson, where 37 residents had been killed in the recent feud. "The town is dead," he reported. "People are afraid to come, and business is at a standstill." He enjoyed riding horseback through the hills and meeting everyone from moonshiners to missionaries, even though the area seemed "filled with men who, if they know nothing else, at least they know how to shoot. . . . I like the mountain people—a fine stock. But not when they get excited." Like everyone he met in Jackson, he carried a gun. The Hargis-Cockrill feud had begun with local political disagreements that grew into a pistol duel between Tom Cockrill and Ben Hargis. Hargis was killed, setting off a string of shootings and deaths. Among the family members and others who jumped into the fray was Curtis Jett, who was eventually convicted of killing a member of the Cockrill family and other feud participants. Spingarn met Jett when he had not yet gone to trial, and through him became acquainted with several members of the Hargis family. Describing them as shrewd and unforgiving, Joel was understandably surprised when several feud participants asked for his help in getting a Carnegie library for the town. They explained their hopes for "a place of culture instead of a place of blood." He also met the local Methodist minister and lectured at his church on poetry and religion. However, the minister advised him to leave town and warned, "You have more chance with a rattle snake than you have with Curt Jett." Indeed, Jett and others had expressed some suspicion that he might be a detective.[5]

Spingarn stayed in Jackson for about four weeks. The evening before he left the hill country for the town of Versailles near Lexington, Kentucky, Curtis Jett took him aside to bid him a warm goodbye. "I was mistaken about you," he said. "My cousin Nancy says you are all right." Jett was sentenced to life in prison in 1903 but was paroled in 1918. When Spingarn moved on to Versailles, he missed the exhilaration of his experiences among the feuding families of Jackson. "The paradox of mountain character meant uncertainty and excitement," he maintained. By comparison, life in the bluegrass country seemed "vapid," and in Versailles "the chief sources of amusement are going to the trains and waiting for the mail." He added, "But all of Kentucky is made interesting by its women." Running low on funds, he asked Arthur to send a money order, which allowed Joel to make a vacation side trip to Estill Springs, Tennessee, and then head back to New York. He hoped to return within a year to the Kentucky mountains.[6] However, the next several summers drew him to European and other US travel, often with his brothers Arthur and Sigmund. There is no indication that he ever published anything related to his Kentucky experiences.

⚖

While Arthur was dealing with a variety of new legal clients, largely in the area of trusts and estates, Joel was becoming known as the outstanding expert on literary criticism in Columbia's Department of Comparative Literature. He was determined to demonstrate that criticism should be concerned with what the author or artist was trying to express, rather than with the standards set forth by the reader or viewer. Shortly after his return from Kentucky, Spingarn and Woodberry founded the *Journal of Comparative Literature*, a quarterly publication with international reach that included "scholars of all lands and contributions printed in the tongues in which they are written." The first issue included essays written in French, Italian, and English.[7]

Spingarn's students were impressed that a tutor so young could know so much. According to Robert M. Gay, a student only six years his junior, "his erudition was almost appalling."[8] Joel also became known for a style of teaching that, according to his friend Lewis Mumford, confirmed "his aversion to tedious pedantry, his hatred of the dry punctilio of habit." Mumford cited a time when Spingarn lectured intensely for a half hour and then concluded: "That is all I have to express on this subject. The class is free for the rest of the hour."[9] Spingarn's student Alfred A. Knopf would remember him as "an unconventional teacher, but an inspiring one. His enthusiasm for the classics, and indeed for any good writing, was contagious."[10]

Satisfaction with his scholarly work did not necessarily carry over to Spingarn's feelings about the directions of the university. In 1902, Seth Low had left Columbia to become New York City mayor, and Nicholas Murray Butler stepped into the presidential role. George Woodberry and Butler immediately butted heads about the prominence and even continuance of the Department of Comparative Literature. Butler sided with the Department of English in the ongoing competition with Woodberry's department for courses and students. Although Woodberry was chair of comparative literature, Butler decided that the courses he taught should be offered under the auspices of the Division of Fine Arts. That unit, housed in Columbia's Teachers College, included widely diverse programs, such as music, architecture, and kindergarten studies. The department budget promised to Woodberry by Low was slashed by Butler. The new president then refused an additional department tutor, although wealthy alumnus Harry Harkness Flagler had offered more than enough money to fund one for several years.

Butler's fury grew when the student newspaper reported on his actions toward the popular professor. He eventually attacked Woodberry in letters he shared with the board of trustees. Finally, Woodberry wrote to Spingarn, "I think my position (as I have long done) impossible." He resigned several days later.[11] Professor Jefferson Fletcher was appointed to succeed Woodberry as head of the department, and Spingarn was promoted from tutor to adjunct professor. Another of Spingarn's faculty friends, renowned composer Edward MacDowell, resigned only a week after Woodberry's resignation. He had become impatient with empty administration promises about developing a first-class music program and was especially frustrated when Butler reduced his music department to a program in the Division of Fine Arts. The treatment of Woodberry was the last straw. "Woodberry was the only spark of the ideal left at the university," he maintained in a long interview published in the *New York Times*. MacDowell labeled his recent years at Columbia "a great disappointment" and the reshuffling of the music department "inefficient and practically useless."[12]

Joel concentrated on his writing and teaching after the departures of Woodberry and MacDowell. In 1908, his revised edition of *A History of Literary Criticism in the Renaissance* was published by Columbia University Press. He was particularly proud of fine reviews not only in the New York press, but from as far away as Chicago, Seattle, and London.[13] To encourage more and better student literary work, he had established and personally funded a competition for three Columbia belles-lettres prizes, one each for best student poetry, short story, and critical essay. Dozens of students competed annually for the $40 or $60 awards from 1906 through 1910. On campus, they became known as the Spingarn prizes.

Both Spingarn brothers mixed their professional concerns with personal pursuits. Arthur's print and literature collection grew as he traveled regularly to Europe, most frequently to London and Amsterdam, and combed through museums, bookstores, and personal collections. While in England, he typically also took time to visit relatives of his mother in Yorkshire. The range of his legal practice also expanded, including one new area brought to his attention by his friend Oswald Garrison Villard. Editor of the *New York Evening Post* and a vocal proponent of liberal causes, Villard was the grandson of famed abolitionist William Lloyd Garrison. He asked Spingarn to take on a civil rights case in 1905. Although race-related issues, legal or otherwise, had not yet been a serious concern to Spingarn, he later recalled that what he learned while trying the case angered him deeply: "You just can't help getting mad. That's all there is to it."[14]

During his early teaching years, Joel also married and started a family. His new wife, Amy Einstein, was the younger sister of his Columbia graduate school acquaintance Lewis Einstein, who had earned a master of arts in history. Shortly after, Lewis had begun his diplomatic career as third secretary at the US embassy in Paris. Their father, David Einstein, was a very wealthy New York and New Jersey woolen magnate and president of Raritan Woolen Mills; he and Caroline Fatman (Einstein) had married in 1872. Their uncle Henry L. Einstein owned the *New York Press*. Twenty-two at the time of her marriage to Spingarn in 1905, Amy was a budding artist and suffrage activist who had traveled several times to Europe with her family. The Spingarns' first daughter, Hope, born in 1906, was soon joined by siblings Stephen (1908), Honor (1910), and Edward (1911).

Not surprisingly, Joel continued to venture into areas beyond his Columbia work and family enjoyment. He soon decided to actively engage with politics. He viewed the political life as a "noble occupation" of practical concern, no less important than those of mental and spiritual concern, such as literature, philosophy, and religion.[15] Unlike his father and uncles, who were committed Democrats, he was a Republican with a high regard for President Roosevelt. After some participation at the precinct level, he accepted the nomination in 1908 as the Republican candidate for the US Congress in the largely Democratic 18th District of New York. He was quickly endorsed by prominent Republicans, including Secretary of State Elihu Root and Secretary of Commerce Oscar Straus. Soon, President Roosevelt added his "hearty endorsement" and pleasure that "such men as Professor Spingarn were becoming interested in public life."[16] Spingarn thoroughly enjoyed the frenetic pace of four or more campaign speeches a night, "whirling from place to place as fast as gasoline could speed me. I attended Catholic bazaars, German literary societies, colored mass meetings, [and] every other function in my district where I was wanted or tolerated."[17]

For many years, Joel delighted in recounting that when a supportive friend spoke for him in a crowded pool hall, someone shouted, "What's he ever done?" The friend hesitated and then noted he had written some very good books, particularly one about the Renaissance. The questioner shouted, "Is he for it or agin it?" Hearing the firm response that "he is one hundred percent for the Renaissance," the crowd burst into cheers: "Hooray, Spingarn!"[18] Although he lost the election, he continued to value the experience. Writing to his former mentor and colleague, Professor Woodberry, he maintained that he felt "no results from this unusual burden of work, except possibly a heightened sense of physical well-being and a temporary ennui at the contrasting tameness of the academic life."[19]

Losing the election did not dampen Joel's commitment to somehow seamlessly combining a scholarly life and a political life. In a lecture at Cincinnati University the year after his defeat, he asserted that "the day of the low-brow politician will soon be a thing of the past. It is not at all extraordinary in England to see college professors sitting in Parliament. Why not in America?"[20]

⚖

By far the most significant early twentieth-century event for the Spingarn family was the purchase by Joel and Amy of a country estate in Dutchess County, New York. They first rented a summer cottage on the property in 1907. Two years later, they acquired the 200-acre estate and its impressive stone manor house. They then enlarged the property with the purchase of 167 contiguous acres. Named "Troutbeck" after a small village in England, the large manor house and the land had been developed since the late eighteenth century by the family of the previous owner, poet Myron Benton. Located between the towns of Amenia, New York, and Sharon, Connecticut, the property was a shallow valley of trees and pastures bordered by hills and wooded ridges. Plenty of brooks and streams crossed through from the Webutuck River. Naturalist and essayist John Burroughs described his friend Myron Benton's estate as "nearer to being the ideal farm and country home than any farm I had ever seen." He found there a feeling of New England and an "over all look of repose and contentment that I believe would be hard to find in the same number of acres anywhere else in the state of New York."[21]

Troutbeck quickly became the place that Joel and Amy considered home, although they continued to maintain a large Manhattan residence on the Upper East Side. Joel added garden areas and a large library wing to the ample main house. Smaller structures on the property became guest houses for frequent visits by family and friends. About 25 miles east of the Dutchess County seat, Poughkeepsie, Troutbeck was not more than 3 miles from the town of Amenia. Trains of the New York Central Railroad made the 85-mile trip from Grand Central Station to Amenia. W. E. B. Du Bois, who first visited Troutbeck in 1916, found the area reminiscent of the Berkshire Hills near his boyhood home in Massachusetts. He noted "the same slow, rocky uplift of land, the nestle of lake and the steady murmur of brooks . . . with a road that rose and dipped and wound and wandered past farm and town to the great world beyond."[22]

Inevitably, the country atmosphere and rural residents soon touched Joel's ongoing desire for not just retreat, but active participation in his community. Eventually, his large footprint in Dutchess County, and especially in the town of Amenia, extended to owning a weekly newspaper, running a charitable club, founding an annual countywide sports festival, and establishing a local American Legion post.

CHAPTER FOUR

Roots of Activism

There was no doubt about what transpired. In the summer of 1907, Pink Franklin, a Black sharecropper in rural central South Carolina, shot and killed a local constable who had entered the tiny cabin Franklin shared with his wife, Patsy, and their son. The constable, Henry Valentine, had arrived at about 3:00 a.m. with a colleague, identified only as Constable Carter. They hadn't announced their names, titles, or mission before breaking into the cabin and opening fire. In response, Franklin shot the pistol he kept by his bedside. The constables also fired. Franklin, his wife, and Constable Carter were wounded. Constable Valentine died instantly.[1]

Things looked very bleak for 22-year-old Franklin. Prejudice against Black people was the natural state of affairs in the rural South, and lynchings had become sport for eager white mobs. Although he hadn't identified himself, Valentine did have an arrest warrant—issued by his brother, the local magistrate—that claimed Franklin had violated the terms of his labor agreement, a contract that held him in a state of peonage. Franklin and his family managed to escape angry locals and find understanding parties who got them to the state prison in Columbia. In a one-day trial six weeks later, with two relatively inexperienced Black lawyers facing a powerful four-man prosecution team and an all-white jury, Franklin's self-defense plea failed. He was quickly sentenced to death by hanging.[2]

Over the next three years as appeals made their way through the courts, the Franklin case grabbed headlines near and far. It was reported in New York, New Jersey, and Connecticut newspapers and dozens of others, including in Salt Lake City, San Francisco, and El Paso. When the US Supreme Court decided against an appeal based on the selection and composition of the jury, an unlikely team of concerned Black advocates, from the accommodating Booker T. Washington to founders of the new National Association for the Advancement of Colored People, pushed at every level of political and popular influence. At the same time, NAACP secretary Frances Blascoer exchanged encouraging letters with Franklin about the organization's efforts. One immediate outcome of the case was the commitment of the NAACP to establish a permanent legal advisory committee. Finally, South Carolina governor Martin Ansel, just days before the end of his administration in January 1911, commuted Franklin's sentence to life in prison. Eight years later, the NAACP claimed victory: it had convinced Governor Richard Manning to pardon Pink Franklin.[3]

The Franklin case was just one of many well-publicized racial incidents during the early years of the twentieth century that grabbed the attention of concerned citizens like Arthur and Joel Spingarn. One national news story of racial strife occurred in Brownsville, Texas, when members of a segregated regiment of Black soldiers at Fort Brown were accused by white townspeople of killing a local bartender and wounding a police officer. The 1906 incident held the public's attention for several years, during which white army commanders confirmed that the 167 Black men of the regiment were in their barracks at the time of the crime. Although their guilt was in great doubt, the soldiers were denied trials by court-martial. Instead, they were discharged and barred for life from military or civilian US government employment by President Theodore Roosevelt—without honor and without any serious investigation. The massive Springfield, Illinois, race riot of 1908—three days of bloody mob violence—also garnered nationwide note. The Land of Lincoln outbreak, occurring north of the more anticipated clashes in southern states, happened when two local Black men were suspected of rape and murder. Hundreds of furious whites attacked all Black citizens they could find, murdered some, and destroyed scores of Black homes and businesses before the Illinois state militia managed to gain control.[4]

However, it was a later newspaper account, this one about Arkansas tenant farmer Steve Greene, that moved the Spingarn brothers to action. Greene had quit working for a landlord who had raised his rent from four dollars to nine dollars an acre in 1910. When the landlord hunted him down and shot at him, Greene ran to his house for his own revolver and shot back, killing his attacker. Chased by a lynch mob, Greene made his way to the Mississippi River and eventually to Chicago. African American journalist and antilynching activist Ida Wells-Barnett spearheaded efforts by the Negro Fellowship

League of Chicago and the NAACP to protect Greene from mob violence, raise money for his defense, and prevent his extradition back to Arkansas.[5] Upon reading of the case, Joel Spingarn immediately donated $100 ($2,970 in 2022). He then wrote to one of the NAACP founders, *New York Evening Post* editor Oswald Garrison Villard, asking if more was needed. Arthur Spingarn, who knew Villard as a good friend, offered to contribute legal opinions. Joel later recalled that although he had seen and heard of many other cases of racial injustice, this one struck him with a sudden and unexpected "strange current of emotion" that prompted him to determine: "I don't care what happens, Steve Greene will never be extradited to Arkansas."[6] Joel later explained that in addition to being horrified by individual acts of brutality, he was also distressed by "the contempt with which cultivated men of the Negro race were treated by the whole body of white citizens."[7]

⚖

Joel and Arthur Spingarn also were aware of well-publicized instances of racial unrest in New York City itself. The new century had begun with hundreds of white and Black residents embroiled in mob violence during the two-day West Side race riot of August 1900. The melee started with the death of a white police officer, who had been attacked by two Black people while attempting to arrest a Black woman. The *New York Tribune* reported that throughout the next night "a mob of white men, which grew from a few score to many hundreds, raged through the district, and negroes, regardless of age or sex, were indiscriminately attacked. . . . The blacks at first offered resistance, but they were so soon outnumbered that they fled without delay."[8]

Arthur's handling of his first civil rights case in 1905 left him with what he viewed as an initial understanding of racial "indecency, inhumanity, and injustice."[9] Joel, on the Columbia campus and with a growing family, was somewhat more distant from the day-to-day realities of the city's Black citizens. Nevertheless, his 1908 congressional campaign and his affiliations with liberal citywide clubs often exposed him to community issues outside his usual sphere of activities.

The Great Migration of Black people from southern states to northern cities had more than doubled from 88,000 during the 1880s to 194,000 in the first decade of the twentieth century. Well into the next decade, that growth prompted great distress and disgust among many white working-class and elite New Yorkers. Historian Marcy Sacks has observed: "On Broadway and Tin Pan Alley, in the workplace, saloons, and tenements, and in the city's police stations and courtrooms, white New Yorkers followed the lead of their southern compatriots in disparaging the viability of black freedom and equality."[10] The general response was strict segregation, according to Sacks:

> Hotels, restaurants, theaters, and bars refused to serve black patrons. Service organizations such as the YMCA organized segregated branches for the black population. . . . Hoping to prevent other humiliating defeats like the one that occurred when the boxer Jack Johnson became heavyweight champion in 1908, the New York State Boxing Association prohibited matches between whites and blacks. And though unsuccessful, in 1910 the New York legislature attempted to reinstate a law banning intermarriage.[11]

Many notable instances of great promise could be found among the new migrants from the South. Growing numbers of talented and educated Black citizens were able to demonstrate a future that would include impressive contributions in literature, art, music, business, and politics. As longtime New Yorkers active in a wide range of community, political, and professional endeavors, the Spingarn brothers would have noticed increasing examples of such Black achievement. Eventually, a number of those talented new residents would become their close friends and associates.

James Weldon Johnson, for example, had left Jacksonville, Florida, for a degree at Atlanta University and then moved to New York City in 1903. He became a published poet and nonfiction author. As a songwriter, he collaborated with his musician brother, Rosamond, and had some early success on Broadway. Still another career began when Johnson campaigned for President Theodore Roosevelt and was soon appointed US consul in Venezuela (1906–1908). He also served in Nicaragua, but then returned to New York City with a determination for racial activism.[12]

Gilchrist Stewart, born in South Carolina, arrived in New York City in 1903 at age 24. He was initially overshadowed by the fame of his father, T. McCants Stewart, a successful Black lawyer and professor who in 1875 had become one of the first Black graduates of the Reconstruction era law school at the University of South Carolina. Gilchrist attended New York University Law School (although he did not graduate) and started a law practice. However, he soon demonstrated he was more suited to politics and racial activism. He joined the new Constitution League, a multiracial civil rights organization, and became active in the New York Republican Committee. His ongoing struggle for Republican planks and resolutions favorable to Black citizens earned him references in the local press as "the negro Republican leader."[13]

But it was his painstaking investigation of the Brownsville, Texas, incident on behalf of the Constitution League that earned him the respect that had eluded his law practice. His evidence and conclusions of great injustice to the Black soldiers prompted a Military Affairs Committee hearing in the US Senate. The findings of that committee, however, fell on deaf ears at the White House, and President Roosevelt refused to revisit his hasty decision to dismiss the accused Black soldiers. Only two of the men were still alive in 1972 when, after the army's new analysis of the evidence, President Richard Nixon issued pardons and honorable discharges to all involved.[14]

Also early in the twentieth century, the works of a notable Black scholar and accomplished author, W. E. B. Du Bois, greatly enhanced many concerned white citizens' understanding of the complex and discriminatory racial circumstances nationwide. Du Bois, in 1895 the first Black person to receive a Harvard University PhD, was a noted sociologist and historian, researching and writing about race contexts and issues while in faculty positions in Ohio, Pennsylvania, and Georgia. His published articles, especially those in the *Atlantic*, found a wide audience among readers who favored meticulous research, literary expertise, and fresh approaches to vital issues. For example, in an 1897 article in the *Atlantic* titled "The Strivings of the Negro People," Du Bois attacked the cruelty of not only discrimination, but also indifference, describing a "veil" between Black citizens and their participation as full US citizens in social, political, and economic interactions. In a 1902 article, "Of the Training of Black Men," he promoted for Black students the liberal college education favored for white youths.[15] This was a far cry from the industrial education model that Booker T. Washington had developed as founder and president of Tuskegee Institute, which trained Black youths for the work most available on their side of the racial divide.

Du Bois was largely familiar to scholars who followed sociological research and analysis, especially his fellow members of the American Academy of Political and Social Science.[16] However, in 1903, the publication of his groundbreaking book, *The Souls of Black Folk*, caught the attention of reviewers and the general public. Part autobiography and part social criticism, the eloquent and stirring volume set forth enduring concepts, such as the "color line" of racial division and the "double consciousness" of Black citizens, who understood themselves through a very different lens than that of others'. A favorable review in the *New York Times* was among the notices of the book's popularity in other New York papers.[17] Joel Spingarn soon reached out to Du Bois for advice related to Black charity work.

⚖

Du Bois and many others became increasingly impatient with the gradual and cautious approach to addressing racial injustice favored by Booker T. Washington and his supporters. Although Washington had long been considered an advocate of Black advancement, he was determined to accommodate white sentiment by favoring only slow and scattered progress toward racial equality. Meanwhile, discrimination, segregation, and violence grew throughout the country. Yet, with political savvy that allowed him access to presidents and congressmen and with his "Tuskegee machine" of powerful white friends and political and press contacts, Washington was impossible to ignore. His presence had loomed large in any counterattempt to push past conservative approaches and effectively demand equal treatment and opportunity across color boundaries. During the early twentieth century, however, determined and increasingly insistent Black people were joined by liberal whites—some with family roots in abolitionist causes and some with socialist political leanings. Many had been briefly encouraged by new "progressive" ideals only to eventually recognize that promises of social and economic betterment were generally limited to whites only. All that was needed for these liberal whites and Blacks to enlist together with a new battle plan for racial justice was a workable organizing framework.

The Constitution League, an interracial organization with funding from white journalist and wealthy self-made businessman John Milholland, was founded in New York City in 1904. According to historian August Meier, the group hoped for at least some tacit support from Booker T. Washington as it aimed "to attack disenfranchisement, peonage, and mob violence by court action, legislation, and propaganda."[18] However, disagreements about conservative versus liberal approaches to various discriminatory ills sowed ongoing discord between the new league and Washington supporters. Particularly objectionable to league proponents was Washington's loyalty to Roosevelt after the latter's decision to discharge the Brownsville soldiers without adequate investigation. Eventually, key activists who had initially respected much of Washington's work began to air their questions about his politically cautious approach, which they viewed as accommodating whites by favoring slow progress toward racial equality. Among those were publisher Oswald Garrison Villard, Mary Church Terrell (the first president of the National Association of Colored Women), and Boston newspaper editor and real estate investor, and the first Black person to be named to Phi Beta Kappa at Harvard University, William Monroe Trotter.[19]

Although the Constitution League remained small and local, it managed some notable successes, especially with Gilchrist Stewart's exposure of discrimination in the Brownsville case. A more militant and widespread interracial effort was launched in 1905 with the prompting of Du Bois. The Niagara Movement, named after the location of its first meeting, began with 29 invited Black conferees from 14 states who would have been considered radical in their uncompromising demands to end all race and color distinctions in every area of personal and public life. Protest and legal action would necessarily be at the forefront of strategies for pushing the Niagara demands.[20] With the cooperation of the Constitution League, the help of the Black press, and the support of well-placed white and Black citizens, the Niagara Movement grew to more than a dozen local branches by the time of its 1906 conference in Harpers Ferry, West Virginia. Marked by rousing speeches and enthusiasm for action, including test cases in the courts and protests against discrimination, the group was poised to take positive steps. While it did have some success in supporting several civil rights cases and energizing local groups, it was also plagued by fundraising issues, internal disagreements, and Booker T. Washington's consistent efforts to destroy it in the Black press and elsewhere. Du Bois later noted that the movement suffered from "my inexperience with organizations" and from meetings in 1907 and 1908 that simply had "less momentum."[21]

Although the Constitution League and the Niagara Movement did not endure, there was ultimately a more positive note about the importance of their groundwork. According to NAACP historian Patricia Sullivan, "During these years, as racial conditions worsened, ideas germinated and personal networks coalesced to provide the foundation of the early NAACP."[22]

The NAACP began in 1909 with a "call," part appeal and part statement of intent, for a national conference "for the discussion of the present evils, the voicing of protests, and the renewal of the struggle for civil and political liberty."[23] The impetus for this was an article in a weekly paper, the *Independent*, about the racially motivated violence in Springfield, Illinois. It was authored by a young self-proclaimed socialist from a wealthy Kentucky family, William English Walling. A graduate of the University of Chicago and Harvard Law School, Walling was soon contacted by Mary White Ovington, a Brooklyn settlement worker, staunch socialist, writer, and activist for women's suffrage and racial justice. Impressed by Walling's article, Ovington met with him at his Manhattan apartment along with liberal reformer and Romanian immigrant Henry Moskowitz. The three "spent the afternoon discussing the race question and deciding on people to form a committee."[24] The trio then enlisted the involvement of Oswald Garrison Villard, who drafted "The Call," published in 1909, exactly a hundred years after the birth of Abraham Lincoln. It appealed for participation in a national conference to address the racial discrimination, disenfranchisement, segregation, and brutality in the twentieth century. The small initial group recruited 60 signers of the document, "people of national reputation," according to Ovington. That impressive group of prominent liberal whites included John Dewey, Jane Addams, Lincoln Steffens, and William Dean Howells. They were joined by college presidents, religious leaders, newspaper editors, and others. Among the seven Black signatories were W. E. B. Du Bois, Mary Church Terrell, and Ida Wells-Barnett.[25]

The outcome of the initial conference was the National Negro Committee of 40 Black and white individuals—largely from New York but also from six other states and Washington, DC. Du Bois later recalled four distinct groups involved: "scientists who knew the race problem; philanthropists willing to help worthy causes; social workers ready to take up a new task of abolition; and Negroes ready to join a new crusade for their emancipation."[26] The committee's platform denounced all oppression and demanded immediate changes toward desegregation, enfranchisement, equal opportunity, and civil rights.

The group's subsequent meeting in May 1910, also in New York City, featured well-known speakers, including Charles Chesnutt, Franz Boas, and Clarence Darrow. Conferees approved a permanent organization to be called the National Association for the Advancement of Colored People, with a national committee, an executive committee, an executive committee chair (William Walling), a treasurer (John Milholland), a disbursing treasurer (Oswald Garrison Villard), and a president (Moorfield Storey). Du Bois did not hesitate to push for an organizational agenda that would include research and propaganda; and within a month, Walling offered him a salaried position to guide publicity from the NAACP offices in the *New York Evening Post* building at 20 Vesey Street. Du Bois left his professorship at Atlanta University and moved to New York as the NAACP's director of publications and research.[27]

⚖

While Du Bois was transitioning from his professorial duties during the summer of 1910, Joel Spingarn was transitioning to a creative combination of academic work in the city, where his townhouse was located just off Central

Park West, and community involvement at his country estate. Their paths first crossed during that autumn when Joel wrote to Du Bois asking advice about how to run the Heart of Hope Club, a Dutchess County charity he had acquired. It provided meals and recreation to the area's poorest Black residents. Du Bois was keen with interest and ample with advice:

> It seems to me that to be successful a club of that sort has got to hitch itself closely on the things that members like and are interested in . . . to smoke and play some games, perhaps drink beer. . . . They would be interested in talks or lectures which have to do with their work or with their race history and circumstances. From this way of combining their work and interests and their legitimate play much might be done to build up club life. . . . I should be very glad to know just how your club is succeeding from time to time.[28]

Joel did stay in touch with Du Bois and soon sent him a copy of his newly published collection, *The New Hesperides and Other Poems*.

It was perhaps inevitable that after he donated to the defense fund for accused Black runaway Steve Greene, Joel would hear more from the NAACP. During the autumn of 1910, Villard convinced him to join the organization, noting that Spingarn's Columbia colleague John Dewey was a founding member. The next month, Joel was elected to the new organization's executive committee. At his urging, his brother Arthur, then sharing a large townhome near Central Park with their parents, soon became an unpaid legal counselor for various NAACP causes, offering advice on civil rights issues and legal actions. Ovington later claimed: "At this time it [the NAACP] gained the allegiance of two of its most disinterested and able workers, Mr. J. E. Spingarn and Mr. Arthur B. Spingarn."[29]

⚖

The Spingarns' motivations for their growing involvement in the cause of racial justice and the work of the NAACP were undoubtedly multiple and complicated. Liberal by nature and perhaps by upbringing, Joel and Amy were increasingly active in the suffrage movement, and Arthur often spoke and wrote to promote health and social lifestyle betterment. Their Jewish heritage, including teachings of one's obligation to others, and a growing sense of shared marginality with Black citizens may have had some influence. However, those perspectives were likely somewhat limited by their family's beliefs and the community-wide assimilation preferences typical of many Eastern European Jewish immigrants of the late nineteenth century and early twentieth. Although they had the financial means to readily contribute to the economic needs of others, they had not shown any earlier substantial charitable support. Personal and professional interests may have had some influence, including Joel's idealism and readiness for new experiences and Arthur's interest in legal challenges to racial segregation and discrimination. Additionally, the NAACP approach fit well with the Spingarns' political and social preferences, noted by biographer Ross as "noneconomic liberalism," a reform emphasis on ending discrimination by creating opportunities that offered fairness and opportunity rather than charity. Poet and novelist Jessie Fauset expressed similar sentiments when she encouraged Joel to "poke us, prick us, goad us on . . . teach us, hammer into us that expediency is not all, that life is more than meat."[30] Fortuitously, the National Urban League, founded in 1910, took up the banner of racial equality in social and economic advancement, while the NAACP emphasized civil rights and equal opportunity.

Du Bois's second wife, Shirley Graham, felt that Joel's career at the very Christian and white Columbia University "rudely reminded him" that he was a Jew, thus prompting him to "turn his attention to the problems of discrimination and intolerance."[31] Indeed, several Jews, in numerical proportion well beyond their representation in the general population, were leaders in the founding of the NAACP, including Rabbi Stephen Wise, Lillian Wald, Emil Hirsch, Henry Moskowitz, and Jacob Schiff. The first NAACP 30-member executive committee included four Jewish people, and nearly half of the NAACP legal committee through the 1930s were Jews.[32] However, David Levering Lewis notes that while antisemitism may have created among Jews a "vaguely kindred past" with African American citizens, that alone does not explain their early twentieth-century involvement and philanthropy regarding racial justice. Additionally, he reminds us that, unlike the later influx of Russian Jews, the immigration of Central European Jews—mostly reform-minded and community-motivated citizens from Germany, Poland, Austria, and Hungary—was largely ended by 1880. Therefore, "families such as the Schiffs, Rosenwalds, Adlers, Flexners, Lehmans, Gruenings, and Spingarns had become decade by decade less distinguishable from other white Americans."[33]

Nevertheless, reformist Jews did typically retain some sense of duty and a desire to help repair the world—expressed in the term "tikkun olam," which is explained by Lewis as "Talmudic prescriptions of charity."[34] Arthur could easily view his work in civil and criminal justice and his involvement in Manhattan civic clubs as undertaking such obligations. Joel, on the other hand, needed to reach beyond his campus world of literary criticism and poetry. At age 25, he wrote to his Columbia mentor, George Woodberry, "I can see how much of my life has been spent in subjecting desire to duty, and how duty has become more and more the master."[35] Only a few years later, he became involved in Progressive Party politics, embraced marriage and family, and began contributing to the NAACP.

The Spingarns and other white Jews affiliated with the founding years of the NAACP were in a good position to bridge the differences of thought that sometimes haunted relations between Protestant white liberals and the Black people they sought to help. Legal scholar Susan Carle notes that white NAACP founders from upper-class backgrounds, such as Villard and Ovington, "possessed a strong sense of social superiority . . . a mix of race progressivism and thinking tinged by racial stereotyping."[36] Undoubtedly, similar suspicions of arrogance could apply to accomplished and highly educated Black people like Du Bois—the exemplar of the "talented tenth"—who often had little in common with Black southerners of the early twentieth-century Great Migration. Thus, the Jews who offered philanthropy and/or leadership in the founding of the NAACP displayed "genuine compassion combined with sage self-interest."[37] They were, according to Eugene Bender, "asked to bear witness as members of the white majority and as members of an historically victimized minority."[38] By 1910, Joel and Arthur Spingarn were on their way to tackling that balancing act in impressive fashion.

CHAPTER FIVE

Goodbye, Columbia

When Columbia University opened its massive new Philosophy Hall with much fanfare in 1910, Joel Spingarn was not impressed. Promoted to the rank of professor the year before, he managed to appreciate only the Amsterdam Avenue exterior. Its expanse of brown brick with ample arches and columns heralded a striking Italian Renaissance style. However, Spingarn refused to conduct his classes in the two-story interior lecture hall of bright white plaster and shiny blackboards, noting that the stark environment was simply not compatible with the more romantic nature of his comparative literature subject matter.[1]

By his tenth year of teaching, and with both independent means and spirit, Spingarn found little remaining at Columbia of what had attracted him as a student and young faculty member. Since the inauguration of President Nicholas Murray Butler, administrative decision-making had steadily shifted toward corporate expedience and away from academic consideration. Spingarn soon observed conditions that "made mechanical efficiency and administrative routine the goal of the University's endeavor."[2] Butler, controlling and imperious, had collected an inner circle of trustees. He favored faculty members who were business-minded and/or socially prominent—mostly wealthy and Episcopalian.

Perhaps ironically, the evolution of American universities early in the twentieth century supported the very professionalization of graduate study that had benefited Arthur Spingarn in establishing his law practice. But Joel lamented that modern seats of learning were designed to create "specialists" and no longer provided "that broad culture and high training which in former days made their influence so potent and so deep." With growing indignation at Columbia, he particularly objected that "our own institutions are governed by self-perpetuating boards of trustees, consisting of financiers, engineers, lawyers . . . , not one of whom is a scholar by profession."[3]

For the outspoken and uncompromising Spingarn, the latest problems with the Butler administration harked back to the treatment and subsequent resignation of his mentor and colleague, George Edward Woodberry. Spingarn's strong support of Woodberry and vocal disappointment at the downsizing of the Department of Comparative Literature undoubtedly had left President Butler increasingly wary of his young faculty member. And, as Butler biographer Michael Rosenthal notes, "It probably didn't help that he was Jewish." The Columbia trustees and Butler were increasingly on guard about being viewed as what one trustee dubbed a "Jew college" due to the large numbers of qualified students who happened to be Jewish.[4] To counter that thinking, Butler had exulted in his 1906 annual report, "Columbia University is a Christian institution and by its charter and traditions its Christianity is truly catholic."[5] When historian Susanne Klingenstein traced the fate of Jewish scholars in American universities, she found that with the changing of presidential administrations at Columbia from Seth Low to Nicholas Murray Butler, "what little liberalism there had been toward the Jews rapidly disappeared."[6] Frederick Keppel Jr., the dean of Columbia College and an undergraduate Columbia classmate of Joel Spingarn, joined Butler and others in their concerns. In 1910, he identified a "Hebrew problem" of too many "ill prepared and uncultured" Jewish students.[7] Already a noticeable rarity as a Jewish professor at Columbia (along with notables Franz Boas and Felix Adler), Spingarn earned additional skepticism when he became a vocal advocate for the rights of Black citizens. By the time the Columbia board of trustees began to seriously consider his future at the university, he was a newly appointed NAACP executive committee member.

Promoted from adjunct to full professor in 1909, Spingarn had managed to continue his steady pace of literary research and writing while increasing his involvement in the Dutchess County community surrounding his country manor. He found outlets for his interests in civic duty and positive action beyond his endeavors as a man of letters. These interests soon led him to ideas for invigorating all citizens of the rural area. His project, Amenia Field Days, sponsored an annual festival of sports and games open to all nearby communities free of admission. Through his Heart of Hope Club, the effort that had motivated him to contact W. E. B. Du Bois for advice, Joel began helping the area's destitute Black population with free meals and recreation facilities. Arthur Spingarn, who suddenly saw very little of his brother, worried that

Joel Spingarn. Courtesy of George Grantham Bain Collection, Library of Congress, Prints & Photographs Division, LC-B2–1234

Joel's new status as a country gentleman might be diluting his efforts at Columbia and his Manhattan civic commitments. In contrast to his brother's expanding family and rural lifestyle, Arthur continued to share a Manhattan brownstone with their parents and stuck closely to his legal practice, local civic clubs, and bibliophile interests.

Joel's off-campus endeavors likely served as welcome distractions that enabled him to avoid dwelling on his frustrations at Columbia. His colleague John Erskine, a popular but somewhat pompous English literature professor, later recalled that during the spring, with a bottleneck of PhD candidates needing faculty to participate in oral examinations in order to graduate, the English and comparative literature departments typically added Friday afternoons and Saturday mornings to the schedule. However, "Spingarn wrote to [English department chair Ashley] Thorndike asking that the examinations for candidates who had written their theses under him be set no later than Friday noon, since he wished to spend Saturdays in the country." That request, Erskine noted, "occasioned sarcastic remarks from professors."[8]

⚖

Differences with faculty colleagues and university leaders were not the only issues confronting Spingarn's professorial life. His scholarship in artistic and literary criticism was highly prolific and widely disseminated in edited volumes and in journals such as the *Nation, East and West, Modern Philology,* and the *Journal of Comparative Literature.* However, his work had become increasingly controversial and was often disputed by other comparative literature academics. He countered the popular notions of American pragmatists like John Dewey and William James when he insisted that creative work need not be measured against stated criteria (impact, precision, public acceptance, and so on). Nor were the usual yardsticks of compelling content and correct form adequate indicators of great artistry. Instead, Spingarn believed that every creative endeavor, especially literature, had its own intrinsic value as artistic expression. Poetry in particular was to be valued for the pleasure it evoked rather than for any instrumental function it might serve.

While this concept of "new criticism" had made some headway in Europe with the urging of Italian philosopher Benedetto Croce, it was disparaged by many top scholars at US universities, including Columbia. Perhaps most worrisome for university scholars was their recognition that the "new criticism" might make obsolete their role as critical analysts of creative works. In a well-received and highly publicized 1910 lecture titled "The New Criticism," Spingarn clarified his approach as seeking common ground between artistic enjoyment and artistic judgment. He insisted that with "judgment erecting its edicts into arbitrary standards and conventions, enjoyment [is] lost in the mazes of its sensuous indecision."[9] Yet his ideas drew objections for their dreamy outlook at a time of growing practicality in university scholarship, teaching, and administration. Spingarn's colleagues saw little to grasp in his rejection of utilitarianism in statements such as "art has performed its function when it has expressed itself."[10]

Issues about Spingarn's departmental role and administrative decision-making came to a head in April 1910 when President Butler decided to fold the Department of Comparative Literature into the Department of English, under the leadership of the English department chair, Ashley Thorndike. Both personal and administrative conflicts were immediate. As Erskine later acknowledged: "Spingarn was brilliant, and Thorndike was solid. Spingarn could speak foreign languages; Thorndike could read them—when absolutely necessary. At no point, neither in special equipment nor in educational theory, did the two men meet."[11]

Spingarn simply refused to recognize the merger, ignoring any department-wide activities, committees, or relationships. He later insisted that "it was like putting a professor of the history of religion in the department of biology and telling him it was only an administrative matter and would not affect his teaching."[12] President Butler, recently returned from a five-month tour of Europe, began receiving complaints from Professor Thorndike about Spingarn's attitude. Thorndike charged that while Spingarn's teaching and research exceeded expectations, his refusal to submit to Thorndike's authority—especially in committee service—created "an undesirable condition detrimental to the efficiency of the Department."[13] When Butler wrote to Spingarn about Thorndike's report, Spingarn was in no mood to sugarcoat the situation. He admitted it was true that he objected to the amalgamation of the two departments, but he insisted that his most important work did not suffer:

> It is not true that I have ever refused to any of my colleagues, in the English
> Department or elsewhere, the benefit of such counsel and scholarship as it is
> in my power to offer them. It is certainly the duty of a teaching scholar to place
> his intellectual gifts (whatever they may be) at the service of his colleagues as
> well as of his students; and, so far as I know, I have never been unfaithful to
> this idea. I confess that my heart sickens at the very thought of administrative
> tasks for which I have neither capacity nor inclination, and I do not propose to
> have the leisure for productive scholarship interfered with by any additional

burdens of this kind; but certainly, every manly and high-minded scholar in the country would sympathize with my refusal to perform such tasks whenever they conflict with my knowledge of my own capacity or my devotion to my scholarly ideals.[14]

Spingarn agreed to meet with Thorndike and attempt to work out some arrangement that suited them both. However, that meeting was delayed by the Thanksgiving and Christmas breaks. After it did happen, in January 1911, Spingarn was able to report to Butler that he and Thorndike had hammered out a working relationship that was satisfactory to both. In the meantime, however, another issue had arisen. And it caused even greater consternation among Columbia's administrative leaders and trustees, eventually resulting in much greater consequences for Joel Spingarn.

⚖

Just prior to his departure for Europe, in June 2010, President Butler had been confronted with a frenzy of press attention in the New York papers and beyond concerning the recent activities of one of the university's most highly regarded professors, Harry Thurston Peck. Peck, who had known Butler since their Columbia student days 30 years earlier, had taught Latin and Semitic languages at his alma mater for 22 years, first as a tutor and later as a faculty member. He was named the Anthon Professor of Latin Language and Literature in 1904 and received a Columbia honorary degree that year. He was the editor of the *Bookman* literary journal, founded in 1895, and in that capacity had created the country's first "bestseller" list. He was also a trustee for the Columbia University Press and an editorial board member of *Munsey's Magazine*. An elegant and popular figure in New York cultural life, he published extensively on his academic subjects and on a variety of popular topics in travel books, children's books, and essays. Likely not to the pleasure of Columbia leadership, his magazine journalism included an article titled "What Women Like in Men."

Divorced from his first wife in 1908 and remarried in 1909, in June 1910 Peck was confronted with a stunning news scoop by the New York *Evening World* headlined "Letters of Professor Peck Figure in $50,000 Suit His 'Dear Tessie' Brings."[15] Segments of letters to Esther "Tessie" Quinn, a stenographer Peck had known for nearly 10 years, followed. Charging breach of promise because Peck had failed to make her his second wife, Quinn had provided her lawyer with correspondence full of endearments like "Dear Love," "My Darling," and "Yours Devotedly Always." A major embarrassment to Columbia University and its trustees, this titillating publicity was not the send-off Butler would have preferred as he was about to embark on his lengthy overseas tour.

The situation festered in trustee meetings, and there were various public defenses and countercharges throughout the summer of 1910. The education committee of the Columbia board of trustees asked for Peck's resignation. Calling Butler "an idol with feet of clay" and "the greatest liar in the United States" in press interviews, Peck seemed determined to ensure that the trustees would not stop at allowing him to resign, but would find a way to terminate his position.[16] This they did in October, shortly after Butler's return from Europe, noting in their resolution that "the best interests of the university require that his official connection with this university shall cease."[17] Soon after, Peck filed a lawsuit against President Butler for slander, based on claims Butler had made in letters and conversations about Peck's mental condition. However, the suit never went to trial. The only legal issue that fully played out was Peck's $100,000 libel suit against the *Boston Post*. A jury eventually awarded Peck $2,500.[18]

Two months after Peck's ouster by the trustees, Joel Spingarn proposed to the Faculty of Philosophy a single-sentence resolution that might have softened the blows Peck was receiving on and off the Columbia campus. He asked for the members to approve the following: "Resolved: That the Faculty of Philosophy place on record its sense of the academic services of Harry Thurston Peck, who was connected with the University for twenty-two years, and was a member of this Faculty from the date of its organization."[19] Although the wording was conciliatory and benign, members of the various departments that comprised the Faculty of Philosophy undoubtedly understood that any mention of Peck with even a slightly positive tone would likely anger President Butler and the Columbia trustees. After little discussion, the group simply voted to table Spingarn's proposed resolution.

Depending on where they sat on the continuum of faculty impressions of Columbia's leadership, professors interpreted Spingarn's proposed resolution in their own ways. John Erskine, for example, was quite friendly with Butler and some trustees; with dramatic exaggeration, he fumed that Spingarn's proposed resolution had "invited his colleagues to make a formal protest on Peck's behalf."[20] Spingarn later reported that President Butler had warned him that he might get into trouble if he pursued his Peck resolution. He recalled responding: "I am not in the habit of altering my conduct because of the prospect of trouble, Mr. President."[21]

Six weeks after Spingarn's resolution proposal, President Butler wrote to his unyielding professor that the Committee of Trustees on Education had decided to recommend to the next meeting of all trustees that his professorship of comparative literature be discontinued at the end of the academic year. Butler's letter mentioned the financial needs of the university and the earlier disagreements with Professor Thorndike about responsibilities in the English department.[22] Butler then met with Spingarn and urged him to write a reply to this notification that might be conciliatory enough to encourage the trustees to reconsider.

Spingarn's January 30, 1911, letter of reply was anything but conciliatory, however. It began by challenging "the legal right of the Trustees to discontinue my professorship on June 30 next (1911)," since his three-year contract as professor would not end until June 30, 1912. He also questioned the university financial issues mentioned in Butler's letter.[23] Although Butler had not mentioned the proposed resolution concerning Peck in his letter about the intentions of the trustees, Spingarn's reply discussed it at length, concluding: "I refuse to believe that this slight act of generous pity, however mistaken it may or may not have been, can have impaired my usefulness to the University or justified serious official displeasure."[24] Finally, he ended his lengthy letter: "I reassert my loyalty to my alma mater; but if security of tenure in the professorship, if fidelity to contract or a sense of obligation to the academic profession, if freedom of speech and conduct do not exist at Columbia, it is right that the academic world should know it."[25]

On March 6, the trustees voted affirmatively on a resolution that "Professor Spingarn be relieved from further academic service from and after March 6, 1911."[26]

☼

Inevitably, Spingarn did not go quietly from Columbia. Even if he had wanted to, the New York press, his current and past students, and many colleagues kept the issue in the forefront for some time. Among his students, future publisher Alfred Knopf was particularly supportive. As a comparative literature student, he had objected to the reorganization that placed that program under the English department, and he viewed his professor's response to the administrative decision as "inspiring and heroic."[27] Lewis Mumford viewed the break as inevitable, noting, "Spingarn fought for professional dignity against bureaucratic convenience; he fought for truth and freedom. . . . He fought for an autonomous faculty against a system that gave all effectual power to the board of trustees and the president."[28] Initially, Joel turned to his brother

Arthur to prepare a lawsuit against Columbia for breach of contract. However, the university did pay him for the unexpired portion of his three-year contract.

President Butler and the trustees were eager to be viewed as basing their decision about Spingarn solely on academic and financial considerations—nothing petty or retaliatory. Butler wrote an article for the *Alumni News* claiming that Spingarn's proposed resolution about Peck had no bearing on his removal. Spingarn then published a pamphlet titled *A Question of Academic Freedom*, which contained all his correspondence with Butler during the 1910–1911 academic year, as well as a chronology of their meetings. It indicated that Butler's claim that he and the trustees knew nothing of Spingarn's proposed Peck resolution by the time of Spingarn's dismissal was highly unlikely. After all, three months had elapsed between that proposal and the trustees' resolution to terminate Spingarn's professorship.

Spingarn was happy to be quoted in the New York press about the drama of his dismissal. He took the opportunity to rail against both Columbia's authoritarian leadership and the faculty who did nothing to push back against it, telling the *New York Times*, "You cannot understand what this case is unless you have some notion of the absolutely unmanly timidity into which the professors of Columbia have been cowed by Dr. Butler." Yet, concerning President Butler, Spingarn insisted that "he and he alone must be held responsible for this arbitrary exercise of power."[29]

Later developments indicated that at least some of those "cowed" faculty members actually were more worried about the direction of Columbia and its leadership than wary of personal consequences for voicing their concerns. One was the outspoken and nationally prominent psychology professor James McKeen Cattell, who had charged in a statement published in the *New York Times* and elsewhere: "The present tendencies in university control do not attract able and independent men. The bureaucratic system by which nearly everything is done by the president is subversive to academic freedom."[30] Shortly after the Peck and Spingarn dismissals, Cattell floated a motion at a Faculty of Philosophy meeting to empower a faculty committee to investigate the manner of appointment and dismissal of Columbia professors. The motion was immediately seconded by revered philosophy professor John Dewey, but it lost by a vote of 16–12. As one unnamed professor noted: "I fancy that no man voted for it who was afraid that he could not easily get a place outside of Columbia."[31] That professor later described Columbia as a "department store" to friends and depicted Butler as "an errand boy to the trustees."[32] In response, President Butler and the trustees immediately discussed ways to force Cattell's retirement. However, it wasn't until 1917 that he was dismissed—an event sparked by his letter to several US congressmen on Columbia University stationery objecting to forced conscription for World War I.

A few weeks after Cattell's dismissal came the shocking resignation of one of Columbia's most prominent and beloved professors, nationally renowned historian Charles Beard. His explanation for his departure was that "the university is really under the control of a small and active group of trustees who have no standing in the world of education, who are reactionary and visionless in politics, narrow and medieval in religion."[33] Upton Sinclair, a former Columbia graduate student, later summarized the situation in his pithy overview of higher learning, *The Goose-Step*: "President Butler's career at Columbia has been like that of a drunken motorist in a crowded street; he has left behind a trail of corpses. In the course of twenty years of office he has managed to expel or force to withdraw some two score men, including most of the best in the place."[34]

Joel Spingarn had kept only slightly abreast of the ongoing Columbia University issues and events after his departure. However, he had been deeply saddened in 1914 when Harry Thurston Peck, financially and emotionally desperate, died by suicide. In a poem titled "Harry Thurston Peck," published shortly after in the journal the *International*, Spingarn blamed and shamed the aggressive president and trustees, as well as the silent faculty:

> This is the man they condemn, this is the man they defile,
> But by all the gods of justice, not his the craft of guile!
> For another poisoned his honor, and all the rest stood still;
> Seven hundred rats obeyed the fox's will;
> Another cast him out, another struck him dead,
> But never a word of protest the seven hundred said.[35]

⚖

Spingarn's scholarly endeavors in literary criticism and poetry did not slow in any way after his departure from professorial employment. Nearly concurrently with his separation from Columbia, his controversial lecture "The New Criticism" was published by Columbia University Press. He was pleased with the many enthusiastic reviews. Unintentionally ironically, the *Chicago Evening Post* declared it "a refreshing sign of vigorous intellectual life in an

American university."[36] The *Los Angeles Herald* applauded it as a "message that is of real value to all lovers of good books and noble literature; a message that is sincere, plain spoken, and vital."[37]

Soon after, a collection of poetry by Joel Spingarn was published as *The New Hesperides and Other Poems*. Subtitled "An American Ode," it was romantic and optimistic about the hopes and dreams of a nation. Secretary of State John Hay, also known to try his hand at poetry, wrote to Joel about it: "I am old and tired, but still I take pleasure in the dreams of other men when they treat noble things—and are well told."[38] The collection garnered widespread approval among reviewers. The *Sewanee Review* summarized the sentiments of nearly all published appraisals by declaring: "These are true poems. . . . Finished workmanship, melody, aptness of phrase, depth of passion and of thought—all are here."[39]

Spingarn's poetry also was published in many anthologies and periodicals, such as the *Atlantic Monthly*, the *Masses*, *Commonweal*, and the *Nation*. Continuing his work on scholarly essays throughout the coming years, he published his ideas about comparative literature and literary criticism in book collections and journals. Among the publications disseminating his contributions were the *Dial*, the *Cyclopedia of Education*, the *Freeman*, the *Journal of Philosophy*, and various essay anthologies.

A decade after Spingarn's Columbia appointment ended, noted literary critic Stuart Sherman of the University of Illinois continued to fret about his approach to criticism. In his published writing, Sherman could not resist unveiled references to Spingarn's Jewish roots by noting his "alien-minded" theories, which stemmed from his "quick Semitic intelligence."[40] Historian Lori Harrison-Kahan views Spingarn as an "early casualty of the academic antisemitism that would erupt in full force in the 1920s, as colleges and universities instituted quotas to reduce the number of Jewish students and English departments, in particular, became notoriously inhospitable to Jewish faculty."[41]

Spingarn's commitment to a life of varied and active achievement, especially in areas of social reform, also grew substantially in the aftermath of the termination of his professorship. In addition to his recent involvement in the NAACP and the community life near his country home, he purchased the *Amenia Times*, a weekly paper he renamed the *Harlem Valley Times*. With his wife, Amy, he became active in the women's suffrage movement in Dutchess County, and he even attempted, unsuccessfully, to convince Theodore Roosevelt to support the cause. He wrote to Woodberry shortly after his dismissal: "If I were to follow my own inclination, I should retire to Troutbeck (the home of my dreams) and forget the sordid Columbia world."[42]

Spingarn clearly enjoyed the role of a country gentleman of wide civic purpose, but his growing commitment to advancing racial justice would form the major focus of his efforts during his years beyond Columbia. His great mentor, Woodberry, wisely advised such larger exertions in a lengthy letter he wrote a month after Spingarn's dismissal. Woodberry first cautioned his younger friend to move past the notion of being wronged and to "put aside from the start any expectation of justice as of happiness. . . . Neither is rationally to be sought as an end in itself by anyone who looks to make a career in society." He continued with advice about future undertakings that presaged Spingarn's work in the coming decades:

> And I do hope (for I am getting prolix) that you will take your present fate easily, and not brood over it or let it obsess you in any egoistic form. Forget it— and Columbia, and go onto other things, things of the great world that knows nothing of Columbia, as if Columbia were but the obscure hamlet where you were born. Oh the power of oblivion in hope is a great power, and this is a good time for you to exercise it, possess it, and use it. Forget, and when your sleep is over, you shall have morning air and a new world.[43]

CHAPTER SIX

Joining by Doing

Shortly after his departure from Columbia became inevitable and always eager for frontline action, NAACP executive committee member Joel Spingarn grabbed an opportunity to establish a New York City branch of the organization. It was the first of numerous local branches that quickly sprang up throughout the country to identify and stop racial abuse and injustice at the local level. It also soon included a New York vigilance committee. Joel called on brother Arthur to provide advice on any legal issues. Arthur's law partner, Charles H. Studin, also joined in the work of the branch. By the summer of 1911, Joel was referred to as the "president" of the New York City NAACP branch, while the New York vigilance committee was headed by lawyer and racial justice activist Gilchrist Stewart. After initial meetings in Joel's midtown Manhattan home, the branch opened an office in a Black Harlem neighborhood; there, Stewart, a stenographer, and sometimes Spingarn worked.[1] Since the vigilance committee accepted donations directly and paid Stewart a small salary, Joel prevailed on Arthur to serve as its treasurer, assuring him "there will be very little for the treasurer to do or hold."[2]

Vigilance committees in the United States already had a long history, including in service to racial justice. Some of the earliest were in the western plains and mountains—expanses of limited government reach where citizens banded together to deal with issues of mining claim protection, cattle rustling, and landownership. By the 1830s and 1840s, vigilance committees in New York City, Philadelphia, Boston, and elsewhere were active in aiding enslaved people to escape from the South and avoid capture and return. Some were highly structured organizations with dues, executive boards, women's committees, and the like. Some sprang up for single issues, including a London vigilance committee organized in 1888 to capture Jack the Ripper. Similarly, some NAACP local branches, especially in the North, grew from groups of citizens who already shared concerns about racial justice. However, historian B. Joyce Ross notes that many others, like those in the District of Columbia and Baltimore, were launched when "specific cases of injustice aroused the black community sufficiently to foster the rise of potent local branches."[3]

In a speech soon after the founding of the New York City branch, Joel Spingarn pointed out that although lynchings and legislated Jim Crow discrimination were not generally recognized as local issues in and around New York City, inequality was nevertheless ubiquitous:

> Colored men and women in this city are confronted every day of their lives with the most galling conditions; they are subjected to insult, passive or active; they are refused service and courteous treatment even in the places where they are guaranteed absolute equality by legal statutes. They have other and more specific wrongs to complain of, including actual injustice in the courts of justice. . . . I am thinking of the studied humiliation imposed upon them daily by three million people.[4]

Aware of the mounting possibility of a long-term system of caste in New York, similar to that in the South, Spingarn concluded that the local NAACP branch would investigate and act on complaints of "discrimination or outrage" to ensure that "laws guaranteeing equal rights shall not forever remain the mere symbols of our hypocrisy."[5]

The small office on 135th Street served as the headquarters for taking reports of racial injustice and planning actions. After less than a year in operation, functioning sometimes as an umbrella for and sometimes as a partner with the local vigilance committee, the New York branch was investigating cases of police brutality, questionable arrests, and violations of civil rights laws. In one case, William Mingo, "a colored man of good character," was attacked by a group of white men while driving his horse and wagon to a stable where most of the teamsters were white. A policeman arrived during the scuffle and shot and wounded Mingo before arresting him. Arthur Spingarn helped to get Mingo an attorney and bail, which allowed him to leave jail and have his wounds treated. Another early investigative action concerned a Black man whose presence on a street in the Bronx astonished two white women, who screamed out in surprise. This attracted some nearby white men, who then beat their Black victim nearly senseless. Fortunately, a subsequent investigation netted witnesses for appropriate court action.[6] The New York branch also investigated cases of racial injustices in nearby New Jersey jurisdictions, such as a murder case in Lakewood where police had arrested only Black people in the area of the crime, even though they had airtight alibis. NAACP leaders were gratified with the reach of their reputation when the lawyer they sent to investigate was greeted by a Lakewood official: "We thought you people would send somebody down."[7]

Arthur and Joel frequently took their work home—or at least into their own Manhattan neighborhoods—to challenge discrimination up close. Although generally viewed as the more publicly reserved but personally friendly brother, Arthur became known for joining young Black people at New York bars and watching for attempts at overcharging due to their race. When that happened, and if he couldn't get a satisfactory explanation from the bartender, he would smash his own glass on the bar and note that the damage costs would equal the elevated charges to the Black patrons.[8] Joel followed the lead of a successful race discrimination case that Gilchrist Stewart brought against the Lyric Theatre in 1912. Joel went with a group of Black men to various other theaters and watched as they were refused seats. After he urged the New York vigilance committee to sue, his testimony in court won the case against those theaters' management.[9] In the coming years, according to NAACP cofounder Mary White Ovington, the New York branch "tested the civil rights law of the state and won many cases against discrimination in theaters and restaurants. White and colored entered into this civic work."[10]

Joel also began speaking tours to create interest in the NAACP, to meet key Black activists, to interact with citizens from political leaders to students, and to increase his understanding of the problems and potential solutions. After eye-opening visits that included several southern states, he wrote to Amy in 1912: "I have seen the negro do almost everything . . . perform a surgical operation, fill teeth, print 300,000 copies of a pamphlet in his own printing plant, work in the factories of the white man, teach and learn." A lunch meeting convinced him that Morehouse College president John Hope was "indistinguishable in looks, culture, instinct, or temperament from an educated white man, and a very fine one at that."[11] Such observations on Spingarn's part indicate to historian David Levering Lewis his "depth, minimal preconceptions, and broad understanding."[12]

The number of NAACP local branches grew to 24 by the end of 1913. They reflected several key premises of the early NAACP, although there was also some overlap of efforts and responsibilities. Legal redress, including investigation and possible court action, became the essential means of dealing with injustices, with particular attention to lynching, disenfranchisement, and residential segregation. Arthur, an unpaid advisor during the NAACP's early years, fielded scores of letters appealing for legal investigations of wrongs to Black citizens. Peaceful agitation and organized demonstrations also were important strategies, as was widely publicizing both the prejudicial treatment of and the successes among Black citizens. Most branches displayed a growing racial diversity, and thus became places that could alleviate the impression of a largely white organization attempting to solve problems for Black citizens. Aware of the optics, Joel noted in one of his earliest speeches to a largely Black audience: "I am tired too of the philanthropy of rich white men toward your race. I want to see you fight your own battles with your own leaders and your own money." Three years later, in 1914, he reiterated in an NAACP annual conference address: "We will stand shoulder to shoulder with you only until you can fight as generals all by yourselves."[13]

⚖

Villard, whose *New York Evening Post* gave the NAACP its early two-room office space, led the initial fundraising and office setup in 1910. Ovington pitched in with office administration duties. They were soon joined by the association's first Black employee, W. E. B. Du Bois. As director of publications and research, Du Bois defined the work of the NAACP broadly: "to make Negroes politically free from disenfranchisement, legally free from caste and socially free from insult." Although his prior research and publications had been detailed and scholarly, he never hesitated to refer to his NAACP work as "propaganda," which simply meant "interpreting to the world the hindrances and aspirations of American Negroes."[14] In the early years, according to Du Bois, the organization was not so organized, but really was "a conference of men and women seeking agreement for common action and finally carrying out the work decided upon by a committee of one or more."[15]

Not unlike the Spingarn brothers carving out their own approaches to local branch work, Du Bois simply moved ahead with his own approach to propaganda. The *Crisis*, an impressive monthly journal founded and edited by Du Bois, began in November 1910 and grew to a circulation of 24,000 two years later. Although some of his colleagues were disappointed that it was nowhere near the NAACP house organ they had envisioned, its reach into Black communities met Du Bois's own goal of spreading news and opinion that would give Black citizens information and a common sense of unity.[16] Good news from throughout the country included educational and athletic accomplishments among Black people, bequests to Black colleges, successful discrimination protests, and political appointments of Black people to key positions. Bad news was rampant enough to require subheadings. A section titled "The Burden" detailed lynchings, largely in the South, but also as far north as Coatesville, Pennsylvania. "The Ghetto" section described residential segregation in various communities. The lengthy "Along the Color Line" described news of note throughout the country related to race issues in politics, religion, science, and art. Early guest editorials were from well-known observers, including reform activist Jane Addams ("The Progressive Party and the Negro") and Black Baltimore lawyer Ashbie Hawkins ("A Year of Segregation in Baltimore").[17]

According to Mary White Ovington, "the most avidly scanned section was the editorial page," a collection of opinions penned, often vented, by Du Bois. "Always scholarly in his effort to print the truth, in expressing an opinion Du Bois could vigorously voice approval or blame."[18] Du Bois's determination that he alone should control what did and did not appear in the *Crisis* often put him substantially at odds with Villard, who had become chair of the NAACP board of directors, and sometimes with active committee member and future board chair Joel Spingarn. Villard, who viewed the *Crisis* as the word of the NAACP, felt it needed oversight beyond its editor. Du Bois, however, fumed that "Villard presumed to tell me how to edit the *Crisis*, and suggested that with my monthly record of lynchings, I also publish a list of Negro crimes." Du Bois saw some hint of race-related differences and later recalled: "To a white philanthropist like Villard, a Negro was quite naturally expected to be humble and thankful or certainly not assertive and aggressive; this Villard resented."[19] It certainly didn't help that Villard's wife, who was from Georgia, refused to allow Black people, even her husband's colleagues or guests, into her house.

Joel Spingarn was drawn to Du Bois's intelligent and cultivated disposition and impressed by his work. But wary of office antagonisms, he often took the role of both caring colleague and frank observer. The two colleagues had similar, often uncompromising temperaments that enabled them to undertake both graceful collaboration and combat. As the *Crisis* editor's closest friend at the NAACP, Joel alone could exercise unbridled candor without risking long-term bitterness. Du Bois, of course, could do the same. Their confidential letters began in 1913 and continued as they shared opinions and ideas about the *Crisis* and aired their differences about office attitudes and interactions. In a 1914 exchange of especially lengthy letters, Du Bois insisted he felt "somehow I have become the object of your suspicion. . . . I very distinctly feel that you doubt my honesty . . . and you are not meeting me frankly and openly as soul to soul."[20]

In a detailed reply, Spingarn began by noting to Du Bois that he counted him among the "men I know and admire." Then, outlining a variety of problematic attitudes, he wrote that Du Bois seemed surrounded by "an atmosphere of antagonism. . . . and even some of your most intimate friends feel toward you a mingled affection and resentment. They have come to feel that you prefer to have your own way rather than accept another way, even when no sacrifice of principle is involved."[21] Du Bois, of course, wrote back in his own defense and disagreed, but their friendship, buoyed by mutual esteem, survived.

Amy Spingarn later recalled that both Arthur and Joel treated Du Bois with respect, but also with "kid gloves." He was, she observed, "a terribly difficult, tricky man." Yet Du Bois's biographer maintained that "a certain affinity of temperament drew Du Bois and Spingarn together . . . a kinship of patrician combativeness and superior culture."[22] Du Bois eventually concluded that while he and Joel "fought each other continually in the councils of the Association," their mutual admiration never wavered. "We disagreed over the editorial power which I should have in the conduct of *The Crisis*, and yet *The Crisis* had no firmer friend than Spingarn."[23]

⚖

In 1913, Arthur Spingarn and Charles Studin officially began their supervision of NAACP legal matters at the local level, as well as reviewing the *Crisis* for potential libel issues. Their early endeavors, strictly on a volunteer basis, were fit in among the demands of the ongoing work for their law firm. NAACP president Moorfield Storey, a highly regarded white lawyer who was serving as president of the Massachusetts Bar Association and was a past president of the American Bar Association, initially took the lead on cases of national consequence. He wrote the first NAACP amicus curiae brief filed in a US Supreme Court case, *Guinn and Beal v. United States*. Decided in 1915, this case challenged a "grandfathering" election statute in Oklahoma that allowed voting by illiterate white men, but not by illiterate Black men. It was won in favor of Black citizens and their rights as protected by the Fifteenth Amendment.

By late 1913, NAACP legal efforts had gained enough weight to merit hiring recent Harvard graduate Charles Brinsmade to lead the organization's new legal bureau. The bureau was to be an information source for branch legal activities, a clearinghouse for branch legal questions and concerns, and a national force regarding legal issues of wider implication. With the oversight of a legal committee chaired by Arthur Spingarn, Brinsmade viewed the legal bureau's role as "the building up of a body of judicial decisions which shall comprehensively state the law on the subject of civil and political rights ... along lines which admit no distinctions whatever on grounds of race or color."[24] He fielded inquiries, investigated possibilities, and wrote reports for the board of directors. However, a little more than a year after his hiring, financial difficulties made it impossible to renew Brinsmade's contract. Spingarn and Studin needed to step up their voluntary NAACP legal work.

Spingarn, Studin, and Brinsmade were fortunate to have courtroom support from Storey, who soon argued a residential discrimination case before the Supreme Court. However, these lawyers highlighted a difficult reality for early NAACP legal efforts. While Black attorneys might handle some local branch work, white lawyers assumed the far more conspicuous roles of leading the organization's legal planning and bringing cases to court. William Hastie, one of the first nationally prominent Black lawyers and eventually a federal judge and a law school dean, later recalled that at that time "there were not ten Negro lawyers, competent and willing to handle substantial civil rights litigation engaged in practice in the South."[25] Historians August Meier and Elliott Rudwick note that studies in the 1920s by well-regarded Black scholars "revealed that black lawyers generally had inferior educations, experienced widespread hostility from courtroom and jury, and faced a Negro public skeptical of their abilities."[26]

The dilemma concerning the appearance of white paternalism surrounding NAACP legal activities would not be resolved for many years. In the meantime, Arthur Spingarn went well beyond lawyering in doing his part toward achieving the NAACP goals. Poet and novelist Langston Hughes noted that Arthur joined colleagues in a large picketing demonstration in Memphis to protest the removal of Black speakers from a national conference of social workers. Hughes concluded, "This was probably the first interracial picket line in the South. ... Arthur Spingarn did not stay cloistered in his law offices, nor was he concerned with court activities alone."[27]

⚖

Although Joel Spingarn had lost his 1908 Republican bid for US representative, he remained active in politics while also initiating various NAACP endeavors and continuing his involvement in the community surrounding his country estate. In 1912, when former president Theodore Roosevelt bolted the Republican Party after losing its presidential nomination to President William H. Taft, he formed the new Progressive (Bull Moose) Party. Joel, who had long considered Roosevelt a friend and remained grateful for his support in the 1908 campaign, was among the first to follow Roosevelt's lead. He quickly became the Dutchess County chair of the new party and took charge of touring and introducing Roosevelt when he visited the area. During the summer of 1912, Joel jumped headlong into ideas and plans for the Progressive National Convention in Chicago, where he would be among the delegates from New York.

Joel was enthusiastic about the Progressive Party stance against big business and political corruption and for social insurance, workplace regulation, and other progressive strides to even a playing field that had ignored individuals and favored giant corporations. Along with Du Bois and others, he believed that such objectives were also ideal for increasing opportunities for Black citizens—especially if combined with a party platform that recognized the aims of racial justice, nondiscrimination, and equal rights. Du Bois later recalled that they "saw a splendid chance for a third party movement on a broad platform of votes for Negroes and industrial democracy."[28] He drafted a platform plank resolution for Joel to offer for Progressive Party approval at the Chicago convention:

> The Progressive Party recognizes that distinctions of race or class in political life have no place in a democracy. Especially does the party realize that a group of 10,000,000 people who have in a generation changed from a slave to a free labor system, re-established family life, accumulated $1,000,000,000 of real property, including 20,000,000 acres of land, and reduced their illiteracy from 80 to 30 percent, deserve and must have justice, opportunity and a voice in their own government. The party, therefore, demands for the American of Negro descent the repeal of unfair discriminatory laws and the right to vote on the same terms on which other citizens vote.[29]

Spingarn arrived by train in Chicago with high spirits. He joined Gilchrist Stewart and 5,000 spectators at a "colored baseball game" where Chicago's American Giants defeated the Cuban Stars. He then dined with Stewart at a segregated boardinghouse that he described as full of "attractive and cultured residents." The next day, he visited Hull House with its founder, Jane Addams.[30] However, when he began informal lobbying with various delegates for adoption of the proposed nondiscrimination plank, his optimistic outlook began to fade. He worried to his wife that "as a matter of political expediency it will not be accepted, and the door of hope will (at least temporarily) be closed on ten million people by the new party!" He also shared with Amy his concern that former president Roosevelt had adopted "a new attitude on the race question."[31]

The proposed platform plank was formally introduced to the New York delegation by Jane Addams and NAACP cofounder Henry Moskowitz. Referred to in the press as the "Spingarn resolution," it was an immediate subject of debate among the delegates, particularly Cornell University professor Alfred Hayes and Hamilton College professor Frederick Davenport. While Hayes supported the resolution, Davenport, an unsuccessful Progressive Party candidate for New York lieutenant governor (1912) and, later, governor (1914), claimed it would reflect poorly on Roosevelt by calling attention to his attitude on the race question. When the New York delegation simply tabled the question, Joel announced: "It is cowardly and not the voice of manhood to take such a position, and the colored voters in the Northern States resent it."[32] Jane Addams appealed directly to the convention's resolutions committee, emphasizing "the inconsistency of pledging relief to the overburdened workingman while leaving the colored man to struggle unaided with his difficult situation."[33]

Du Bois correctly summed up the failure of the resolution: "Theodore Roosevelt would have none of it."[34] Determined to court some southern Democrats, Roosevelt had heeded the warning of one of his key strategists, Louisiana politician John M. Parker, who insisted that southerners "cannot and will not under any circumstances tolerate the negro."[35] Soon to be nominated as a third-party presidential candidate if all went smoothly at the Progressive Party convention, Roosevelt searched for a way to accommodate both white southern delegates, whose states largely prevented Black voting, and northern Black voters, who had generally supported him. In a lengthy letter just prior to the convention, he had pronounced his decision that Black delegates from northern states could fully participate, while Black people from southern states would be excluded. Something for everybody—or at least for everybody white. The former president was careful to explain that this compromise ultimately would help the health and unity of the Progressive Party, which, once in power, would eventually be best for Black citizens. As historian George E. Mowry observes, Roosevelt claimed that "the only man who could help the Negro in the South was his white neighbor," and the Progressive Party "would put leadership in the South into the hands of 'intelligent and benevolent' white men who would see that the Negro got a measure of justice."[36]

Roosevelt's idea about which delegates would be seated was approved by the credentials committee. However, the compromise ultimately proved to carry little weight with southern voters, since they objected to the involvement of northern, as well as southern, Black voters in electing a president. For Joel, whose friend Lewis Mumford viewed him as once "under the spell of Theodore Roosevelt," the convention outcome was a bitter pill indeed.[37] He returned with plenty of reason for discouragement with partisan politics and soon resigned from the Republican Club of New York. He also soon contacted another Roosevelt, the 31-year-old New York state senator Franklin D. Roosevelt, about a legislative proposal to outlaw marriage between the races.[38] The outcome was more encouraging this time. New York was one of 10 states that never enacted antimiscegenation laws. Interestingly, Spingarn remained loyal enough to progressive ideals to return as a delegate to the Progressive Party convention in 1916.

Back from Chicago, Du Bois vented his own dismay through various interviews and quotes in the *Crisis*. He widely broadcast support for Democratic candidate Woodrow Wilson. NAACP board chair Villard, who considered himself a personal friend of Wilson, approved.[39] However, the machinations that paved the way for Wilson's election proved aggressive on political success but absent of equal rights commitment. Wilson, born in Virginia and raised in South Carolina, had been known to tell jokes about "coons" and "darkeys," and he had ridiculed Roosevelt's earlier appointment of a qualified Black man as collector of the Port of Charleston.[40] After his election, he took steps to further racial inequality through increasing segregation and shrinking job opportunities for Black people. When he agreed to the segregation of federal offices and hiring practices, he justified it as a "plan of concentration" that would separate Black workers into places where they were "less likely to be discriminated against."[41] As expected, they soon were also less likely to be retained or promoted. The Progressive Era, which held such promise for economic and political inclusion of those being left behind, had proved to be limited to progress for whites only.

The NAACP moved to try to reverse the segregation of federal employees, first in an open letter to President Wilson from Villard, Du Bois, and Storey. In it, they charged that Black people were being treated "as if they were leprous." It was widely circulated to the press and to members of Congress.[42]

Mass meetings and protests at NAACP branches followed. Villard tried tirelessly to get a meeting with Woodrow Wilson on the subject, but the president was not interested in hearing of the Black cause. When Wilson did finally invite Villard to lunch in October 1913, he admitted that the southern politicians had won him over. Villard concluded and often inserted in speeches at mass meetings that "the President's philosophy is wrong, his democracy is gravely at fault. . . . nowhere do we find any indication that his democracy is not strictly limited by the sex line and the color line."[43]

The attempted intervention in political decision-making, while unsuccessful, reenergized the NAACP's Washington, DC, branch and introduced the possibility of NAACP action at the national level. Soon, the *Crisis* began publishing the voting records of US Congress members on bills negative to Black citizens, as well as surveying national office candidates on their views on civil rights. Joel Spingarn concluded from the experience that "reformers and prophets are always ahead of politicians."[44]

⚏

The discouraging actions of the Wilson administration were just one arena of growing dismay among those fighting for increased racial justice and equal treatment. Lynchings increased from 63 nationwide in 1912 to 79 in 1913, noted by Langston Hughes as "an average of more than one mass murder a week."[45] Residential segregation ordinances, inaugurated in Baltimore in 1910, quickly spread to cities in the South and Midwest. Bills to outlaw racial intermarriage were introduced in the legislatures of at least a half dozen northern states between 1911 and 1915. The American Bar Association began restricting membership to only white lawyers in 1912.[46]

While the NAACP had always committed to legal challenges as a key strategy toward racial equality, its efforts in that area escalated in the wake of the discouraging realities of continuing segregation, disenfranchisement, and unequal justice. Arthur Spingarn, Charles Studin, and others working pro bono and when available needed to be molded into a more formal structure—one that would not only respond to immediate issues, but also develop test cases to aggressively attack injustice over time. The path to a new and stronger legal structure included slowly folding the local vigilance committee legal work into a legal committee at the national level. Spingarn became the national legal committee chair in 1914 and continued in that position until 1940, while also serving as an NAACP vice president and maintaining his practice in trusts and estates at 55 Liberty Street.

As the vigilance committee began to restructure and shrink, Gilchrist

Stewart's role in the NAACP's legal activities was all but eliminated. To his bitter disappointment, he was not included on the new national legal committee, which, with only one Black lawyer, was easily open to charges of tokenism. He fumed to Joel Spingarn that "for work among colored people, it is necessary that colored agencies should be in control."[47] However, even Du Bois recommended to Arthur Spingarn that Stewart, who retained his own law practice on Broadway in New York City, should be only an outside lawyer hired on a case-by-case basis. By late 1913, the vigilance committee legal work ended, and the NAACP was no longer working with Stewart. Joel contributed from his personal funds to cover the last few months of Stewart's salary.[48]

Arthur's interests and activities did not stop with guiding NAACP legal actions while also actively working with his own clients. Still unmarried prior to World War I and living with his parents in a large townhome near Central Park West, he took time to study and write about New York City sanitation and hygiene issues while a member of the New York Social Hygiene Society. He was particularly concerned with sexually transmitted diseases among poor and homeless people, and he wrote a large reference volume, *Laws Relating to Sex Morality in New York City*, published in 1915. Intended for social workers and law enforcement agencies, the book explained and analyzed legal offenses, arrests, and punishments relating to rape, abortion, adultery, bigamy, prostitution, incest, pimps, and numerous other concerns of sexual morality. Arthur had found the laws related to sex and morality inconsistent and messy, and he wrote that he hoped "the grouping together for the first time of these laws may lead to their careful and scientific study."[49] Joel sent his brother enthusiastic congratulations on "your first book" from his home in Amenia. He concluded, perhaps with a smile: "Even to an outsider, it looks a most workmanlike piece of work."[50] After its publication, Arthur lobbied New York assembly members in Albany for stricter legislation in several areas related to sexual morality.[51]

Also during the early days of his NAACP involvement, Arthur expanded on his long-standing interest in books and prints, which had initially emphasized works of the Elizabethan and Tudor periods. His bibliophilic commitment, which would last for the rest of his life, had already prompted searches in various bookstores, churches, libraries, museums, universities, and private collections in the United States and Europe. Now, he started a collection of important literature by Black authors, poets, songwriters, pamphleteers, essayists, folklorists, and others. His unflagging quest for items of interest, ancient and contemporary, was both a personal enjoyment of the challenge of amassing important works in one place and a determined pride in widely sharing the reality of Black cultural accomplishments throughout the world. In a paper he read at a church service, he reminded his listeners: "The ignorance in this country among all groups—white and colored—concerning the cultural achievements of the Negroes is profound. Millions of literate white Americans are quite unaware that any Negro has ever written a book."[52]

Elsewhere, he explained that initially he wanted only a small, exemplary collection:

> I intended to assemble a small representative group of books that I could show to doubting friends who questioned the intellectual capacity of the Negro . . . to those people who were continually saying to me, "If the Negro has the capabilities you insist he has, why hasn't he published books to prove it?" And my answer was to be "He has, and here they are."[53]

However, Arthur discovered in himself "a mania for completeness." Instead of collecting some examples, "I found myself undertaking the impossible task of acquiring *everything* the Negro had written."[54] By 1917, he was selling some of his earliest prized items by white authors, including first editions of works by Poe, Thackeray, Dickens, and Shelley, and autographs by Charlotte Brontë, Elizabeth Barrett Browning, Walt Whitman, Samuel Johnson, and others.[55]

Like his brother, Joel was determined to correct and elevate the national image of Black citizens' achievements. In 1913, he endowed the Spingarn Medal, an annual award granted by the NAACP to an individual of African descent who attained the highest level of honorable achievement in any field. His father-in-law, David Lewis Einstein, had died in 1909, and his mother-in-law died not long after. When the Einstein estate of nearly $4 million was settled among Amy and her two siblings in 1913, the financial strength of Joel's family provided ample opportunity for both good works and a good life.[56]

Elected chair of the NAACP board of directors in 1914, Joel also undertook numerous endeavors well beyond his work for racial justice. As his friend Lewis Mumford recalled, he was "equally at home in a garden, a library, an office, or . . . a battlefield."[57] In Amenia, he was growing the circulation of his weekly paper, the *Harlem Valley Times*, and continuing to indulge his community spirit in the benevolent Heart of Hope Club and area-wide field days. With Amy, he took part in the various interests of their four young children, and he was beginning a serious commitment to planting and gardening. Such activities suggested to biographer Marshall Van Deusen "his peculiar desire to combine *noblesse oblige* with folk democracy."[58] Additionally, during 1913–1914, Joel was the author of nine journal articles, reviews, and book chapters concerning literature and criticism. He even tried his hand at fiction in a medieval love story that he characterized as "a little lyric" with an updated setting at an American university.[59] Although he could get to his Dutchess County estate by train from Grand Central Station, Joel sometimes motored from Manhattan in his Stutz Bearcat.[60]

Given the range and diversity of interests of both Arthur and Joel, it was perhaps expected that each was viewed in a variety of different lights by friends and associates. Mary White Ovington, for example, had known Arthur for nearly 20 years when she described him in connection with his NAACP legal work: "so quiet and says so little." Yet others saw an outgoing and jovial nature that led one interviewer to note his "vivacity and charm." Historian David Levering Lewis labeled him as "Joel Spingarn's ebullient brother" and as Joel's "less-glamorous brother." According to a longtime friend, Arthur struck acquaintances as "the kind of fellow—if you spent ten minutes with him you would love him."[61]

Likewise, Joel demonstrated at various times and circumstances the thoughtful intensity of a scholar and the outgoing reach of a man of action. Sociologist Lewis Mumford, who also had a home in Amenia, described him as "slim, erect, austere, with dark brown eyes that would ignite at the first spark of thought." His brother-in-law Lewis Einstein viewed Joel as "craving for action" and in rebellion against "his own natural academic inclinations."[62] As the Spingarn brothers took on greater NAACP leadership responsibilities, their varied interests and demeanors were well suited for their diverse roles in the growing struggle for racial justice and equality.

CHAPTER SEVEN

New Tactics for New Abolition

The NAACP national legal committee eagerly sought test cases aimed toward Supreme Court rulings that could end segregation, discrimination, and other barriers to racial equality. As its chair, Arthur Spingarn also monitored civil rights litigation that involved other organizations or lawyers not associated with the NAACP. The idea was to understand and learn from other sources. However, one legal analyst determined, "The NAACP wanted sufficient involvement to allow it to take credit for as many civil rights victories as possible."[1] Most cases that rose to NAACP attention were brushed aside on technicalities, lack of evidence, or other problems. For example, *McCabe v. Atchison, Topeka & Santa Fe Railway Co.* looked like a promising challenge to Oklahoma's "separate but equal" railway accommodations law. However, a key factor in the 1914 Supreme Court decision in favor of the railway company was that the appellants had not actually traveled or requested travel or services on the railroads involved.

Soon after that decision, Joel Spingarn, the chair of the NAACP board of directors, wrote to Arthur with an idea for taking the matter into his own hands by planting an airtight Oklahoma test case. Characteristically, he suggested that he could play a key role by "going down to Oklahoma and, with a reputable and trustworthy colored man, touring the state for the purpose of showing that the white man can get sleeping and dining accommodations on the railroads and the black man cannot." He proposed using a small camera to collect evidence "to show the discrimination that the colored man will suffer." Less than two weeks later, Joel set out across Oklahoma by train with a Black traveling companion, Scott Brown, a member of the Muskogee, Oklahoma, branch of the NAACP. Since Brown was light-skinned, Joel had him ask the conductor outright whether he, as a Black man, could ride in a car often reserved only for white passengers. After Brown was not denied a sleeping car berth or subjected to other discrimination in three days of travel, Joel wrote home to Amy that the experience "seemed a fiasco."[2] Eventually, Brown did experience some railway discrimination, but by that time, World War I had stalled NAACP legal work on such cases. The test case strategy, a success for the New York branch when Joel had demonstrated racial discrimination in theater seating, could be difficult, costly, and uncertain. However, as legal scholar Susan Carle finds, the approach served as "a multifaceted strategy to achieve publicity, organization building, and litigation goals."[3]

Arthur Spingarn, well aware that a wide variety of legal issues continually came to the attention of the NAACP, frequently clarified that the national legal effort should be restricted "to establishing precedents and testing new laws."[4] As that work drew more attention, he became increasingly frustrated that "every colored man or woman in the country who has been cheated or wronged or lost a position or wants a promotion assumes that through our association he can obtain the end he desires."[5] Joel regularly brought potential cases to Arthur's attention, but more often than not, further examination indicated they should not be pursued. However, several involving college admissions led Arthur to conclude that "there is evidently an epidemic of this discrimination in the universities, and the Association must take some positive stand as to what it intends to do."[6] That concern became one of many back-burner issues that simmered until they were deemed ready for direct and optimistic legal challenge.

After the success of *Guinn and Beal v. United States* in striking down voter disenfranchisement, NAACP lawyers began searching for just the right case to address the growing practice of residential segregation. Du Bois noted in the spring of 1915: "The field of the Association's activities against segregation ordinances extends from Birmingham, Alabama, to Harlem, New York, and as far west as St. Louis. . . . The Louisville [NAACP] branch has now engaged one of the best law firms in the city to carry a test case to the United States Supreme Court."[7]

The Louisville, Kentucky, test case regarding residential segregation began in earnest shortly after a city ordinance passed in the spring of 1914, which required that white and Black citizens live on separate blocks. The block-by-block idea was an attempt to meet the Fourteenth Amendment concept of equal protection. Whites could not move into majority-Black neighborhoods, just as Black families could not move into majority-white neighborhoods. Concerned local citizens soon began to organize around the issue, and within

Arthur Spingarn. Photograph by Carl Van Vechten, Yale Collection of American Literature, Beinecke Rare Book and Manuscript Library; used with permission of the Van Vechten Trust

months, Joel Spingarn and several staff members arrived to speak to large groups and grant official NAACP recognition to a new Louisville branch. Arthur and his legal team immediately began strategizing for a test case that could eventually make its way to the Supreme Court.

By November, William Warley, a Black man and NAACP member, offered to purchase a lot in a predominantly white block from a white real estate agent, Charles Buchanan. Warley's carefully worded contract stated that both men understood that Warley was purchasing for the purpose of building a home where he would reside. Furthermore, no payment or deed would be exchanged unless Warley had a legal right to occupy the property. Buchanan agreed to the offer and terms, and when Warley did not complete the purchase in an area that barred his residence, Buchanan filed a suit against Warley to determine the validity of the ordinance. In essence, according to historian George C. Wright, the NAACP had developed an unusual test case where ultimately "a white man, backed by the NAACP, called for the outlawing of the ordinance; a black man, represented by the city attorney, claimed to be fighting to uphold the ordinance."[8]

The Jefferson County Circuit Court upheld the constitutionality of the ordinance, and the Kentucky Court of Appeals agreed. By the late summer of 1915, Arthur Spingarn announced that the Louisville segregation ordinance would be appealed to the US Supreme Court. NAACP president Moorfield Storey would argue for the plaintiff. As later noted, the case had "all the elements of the early NAACP's test case strategy: national office control, invocation of the patrician Moorfield Storey to gain legitimacy before the high court, and, most tellingly, the engineering of a factual situation that presented the legal issues at stake in the best light possible."[9]

In November 1917, the Supreme Court delivered its unanimous decision in *Buchanan v. Warley*, overturning the Louisville ordinance. Only Justice Oliver Wendell Holmes hesitated a bit, fretting that the case seemed "manufactured."[10] Storey claimed that "it is the most important decision that has been made since the Dred Scott case, and happily this time it is the right way."[11] This decision is well remembered as achieving a victory for Black citizens by demonstrating that a residential segregation ordinance interfered with the property rights of a white citizen.

⚖

Consistent with his enthusiasm for personally developing evidence of discriminatory treatment on Oklahoma railways and elsewhere, Joel Spingarn jumped into his NAACP board chairmanship with a passion for active—sometimes frenetic—participation. He began rounds of tireless travel, largely at his own expense, to speak to large crowds and small groups about racial injustice and the work of the NAACP. Langston Hughes recalled: "Within a month, Joel Spingarn held conferences and addressed meetings in eight cities, soliciting support, recruiting members, and creating good will." His efforts paid off because "his charm and culture enabled him to interest others like himself in its [the NAACP's] objectives—persons with influence in high places or with access to the media of public opinion."[12] William Sinclair, who had been enslaved and was now a Black physician active in the founding of the NAACP, lauded Joel for demonstrating a "happy combination of conservatism and radicalism—conservatism on non-essentials and radicalism whenever principle is involved."[13] With his wife and four young children at home during this time, Joel found it expedient to fill his days on the road to the brim so he could return to his Amenia estate for longer stretches with his family.

He spoke of the need for a "new abolition" with reference to the earlier uncompromising intensity of activists determined to end slavery. But according to biographer Ross, he decided to focus his efforts on what Black citizens could do for themselves rather than wait for the benevolence of whites. The new abolition movement "would seek to organize blacks and their 'friends' that they might actively, though peacefully, demand the black man's rights."[14] From 1913 through 1915, with advance planning and publicity support from NAACP staff secretary May Childs Nerney, Joel traveled to more than 30 cities, including Denver, Omaha, Chicago, Pittsburgh, Cincinnati, and Minneapolis. In Cleveland, he addressed a crowd of 2,500.[15] Often with two or three engagements a day, he spoke in venues large and small, met with local NAACP branch members, and gathered with concerned citizen groups that might help to start new branches. Historian David Levering Lewis concludes: "With his gleaming black hair, long, dark face, and intense eyes that drew men and women everywhere into his discourse, Spingarn propagated the faith on black and white college campuses, in churches of every denomination, men's and women's clubs of high and low standing—among anyone to whom the new abolitionism brought confidence and commitment."[16]

Although his white audiences were sometimes sparse, he visited both predominantly white colleges, such as Ohio State University, the University of Cincinnati, and Macalester College, and historically Black colleges, including Fisk University, Atlanta University, and Benedict College. While visiting Washington, DC, he launched the first NAACP college branch at Howard University. During this period of new abolition travel, he also reached into his scholarly portfolio to hold seminars in literary criticism for advanced students at two southern white colleges, the University of North Carolina and the University of South Carolina.[17]

In his speeches aimed at exposing injustices and organizing for change, Joel was far more insistent and strident than many expected. He encouraged

Black people in bloc voting, as well as in protest and agitation. Much to the disappointment of influential NAACP founder Oswald Garrison Villard, Spingarn also expressed his negative feelings about the gradual and accommodating ideas of Booker T. Washington toward the advancement of Black people. Referring to Washington's commitments to his conservative friends, politicians, and benefactors, Spingarn insisted to a Memphis audience that this put Washington in a "delicate position" and left him unable to "fight against Jim Crowism, segregation laws, and insulting inter-marriage laws." He suggested that Washington's friends "should join hands with those who stand with Du Bois in the battle against the erection of a monstrous caste system in this country."[18] His public objections to Washington were not always widely shared by Black or white factions, however. After a speech in Chicago, an article in the *New York Age* contended that his attack on Washington demonstrated "one of the inborn propensities of a certain type of white people who profess to have great ambition to lift up the Negro, but begin by attacking a colored man or trying to pull him down as soon as he reaches a certain degree of prominence."[19]

Combined with other efforts, including extensive travel to western states by W. E. B. Du Bois and Supreme Court victories in cases of disenfranchisement and residential segregation, Joel Spingarn's speaking tours bore fruit in helping to expand the reach and membership of the NAACP. The number of local branches grew from 24 in 1913 to 63 in 1916, and 4 college branches were established. Membership increased to nearly 10,000 during that time, while *Crisis* subscriptions reached more than 35,000.[20]

In addition to his busy schedule of NAACP activities and Amenia community involvement, Joel continued to join Amy in speeches and protest meetings in support of women's suffrage, exuding conviction and urgency. At one meeting after the start of World War I, he pointed to the US democracy as the envy of much of Europe, but more needed to be done: "Shall we say to the men of Europe, 'No, we don't really believe in democracy. We believe in half democracy'? There is no real democracy unless the women get a chance to help in making the laws." Two months later, Arthur joined a group of pro–women's suffrage New York lawyers to speak at the same Manhattan venue.[21]

The early years of the NAACP were not only a very active time for the brothers, but also a time of personal financial abundance from several sources. The multimillion-dollar estate of Amy's father, David L. Einstein, settled in 1913, with Arthur Spingarn representing the trustees. The next year, following the death of their uncle Samuel Hersch Spingarn, Joel and Arthur were each bequeathed $71,013 (equivalent to almost $2 million in 2022).[22]

The NAACP was growing not only in members and branches, but also in areas of involvement. The lynching of Black people by white mobs continued to draw attention, especially with regard to the prospect of federal anti-lynching legislation. However, neither President Taft nor President Wilson was willing to add White House support to get it passed. Bills that came to Congress were pushed by the NAACP but stopped by the powerful southern bloc.[23]

Also disappointing was the result of the NAACP campaign to bar showings of the film *The Birth of a Nation* (1915). Depicting Black slavery as a noble time for all and the Reconstruction era as an occasion for corrupt and criminal Black people to undermine the good works of the Ku Klux Klan and other whites, the movie drew immediate attention. Throughout the late winter and spring of 1915, Arthur Spingarn collected copies of city ordinances throughout the country governing the exhibition of films, and he worked to demonstrate to local authorities that they could ban the movie in their cities. He also considered a proposal to undertake a historically correct counterdocumentary that would create "a vivid and impressive restatement of a great chapter in American history."[24]

NAACP branches staged protests, while the national office pressured the National Board of Censorship to stop screenings and start legal action against director D. W. Griffith. Joel Spingarn, Du Bois, and Villard led a delegation of 500 citizens to press New York City mayor John Mitchel to shut down the film's opening there. Most of these efforts were unsuccessful, but scattered victories did happen. Some local authorities managed to refuse permits to theaters wanting to show the film, including in Minneapolis, Chicago, Cleveland, Denver, Des Moines, Albuquerque, Providence, and Wilmington, Delaware. In several other cities, objectional scenes were cut before showing. Board chair Spingarn took pride in the united energy displayed by Black people throughout the country in confronting "this attack on their character and their place in history."[25]

⚖

On the heels of his new abolition speaking tours, and as his brother Arthur was preparing the Louisville residential segregation case for Supreme Court arguments, Joel took the first of several leaves from the NAACP to attend civilian training camps that supported a national preparedness movement for possible US entry into World War I. In the summer of 1915, he attended the first and largest such camp, which had been established in Plattsburgh, New York, on Lake Champlain. It was primarily populated by well-to-do, college-educated white men from New York and Chicago. They paid their own expenses and stayed for 30 days of improving physical fitness, training in arms, drilling in military formation, and pursuing other areas that might help build a cadre of men ready to become wartime officers.[26] It was a rigorous regime that brought Joel to near collapse when he returned. However, still eager to test the limits of his endurance and passionately patriotic, he attended a similar camp at Fort Oglethorpe, Georgia, the next year and later drilled at various New York armories. When not active in military preparedness, he read voraciously on military tactics and served on the Dutchess County Home Defense Committee.[27]

During this time, Joel frequently called on Arthur to look into issues occurring at the main NAACP office, including those far afield of his legal commitments. A typical example involved Du Bois, whose independence and range of work often had invited questions and clarification. In a letter in early 1916, Joel asked Arthur to "get together with Du Bois and talk over the exact delimitation of his work and time.... Just how much of his time he owes us, and what kind of work outside of the *Crisis* he will undertake."[28] Arthur was generally accommodating, even when requests were not at all within the scope of his NAACP legal work. However, he also maintained his own clients and his own interests, especially his travel and correspondence in pursuit of rare works by Black authors, poets, and composers for his growing collection. Since the publication of his book on New York laws related to sex and morality, he also had become active in lobbying various assembly members in Albany about amending and/or passing relevant laws that might address problems he had uncovered.[29]

⚖

James Weldon Johnson had moved to New York City after first teaching school and editing a newspaper in Florida and then serving as the Roosevelt-appointed US consul in Venezuela and Nicaragua. He was surprised to receive a letter from Joel Spingarn early in the summer of 1916. It invited him to join white and Black citizens at a three-day meeting in August at Spingarn's estate in Amenia to discuss questions of race relations. At the bottom of the invitation was a hand-scribbled note, "Do come," from W. E. B. Du Bois. Intrigued and curious, Johnson quickly responded that he would attend.[30]

Johnson's invitation was one of nearly 200 sent to Black and white men and women noted as leaders in race issues. The proposed meeting at Amenia represented Spingarn's idea of attempting to unify conservative and liberal approaches to pushing toward racial justice. Johnson, with his Theodore Roosevelt diplomatic appointments, was viewed as somewhat closer to the conservative end of the spectrum that had attracted followers of Booker T. Washington. Washington had died in November 1915, and Du Bois and Spingarn saw an opportunity to bridge differences between those favoring slow progress and those calling for immediate action. They planned a meeting that was not in any way an official NAACP event. It was, according to Du Bois, an occasion during which individuals "of all shades of opinion might sit down, and rest and talk, and find agreement so far as possible with regard to the Negro problems."[31] They invited many conservative individuals who had worked with Washington, as well as those considered radically militant. Emmett Scott, Tuskegee secretary and Washington confidant, accepted the invitation, as did prominent Black mathematician and essayist Kelly Miller and stormy activist William Monroe Trotter. Presidents Wilson, Taft, and Roosevelt received invitations. They all sent regrets, but also messages of goodwill.

Fifty individuals committed to racial justice and equality gathered at the 200-acre Spingarn estate, Troutbeck, which was dotted with rented sleeping tents, cots, tables, and chairs for the occasion. To Du Bois, it was the ideal setting: "Its great trees bending over the running brook" created "a sense of friendship. . . . One could trudge from the more formal home and lawn, by lane and fence and rise and fall of land." It also reminded him of his western Massachusetts roots: "I knew it was mine. It was just a long southerly extension of my own Berkshire Hills."[32] Among those attending were prominent names in education, activism, and a variety of professions, including Morehouse College president John Hope, historian Carter Woodson, lawyer Ashbie Hawkins, novelist Charles Chesnutt, suffrage activist Mary Church Terrell, clergyman Francis Grimké, and educators Lucy Laney, Nannie Helen Burroughs, and William Bulkley.

The opening session was an address by New York governor Charles Whitman. It was followed by three days of planned sessions and invited discussions about what needed to be done and what could be done concerning problems familiar to all, including discrimination, law enforcement, voting, and lynching. There was time for swimming and rowing in the lake, hiking, playing tennis or croquet, and chatting with friends. The occasion also introduced Amy Spingarn to many for the first time. They were impressed by her commitment to both racial and gender equality and her gracious welcome to new friends. In a congratulatory note to his brother soon after, Arthur Spingarn declared the gathering "the most interesting group I have ever been with" and added that several attendees had already come to his office still enthusiastic about the results.[33]

There had been no attempt at a unanimous final statement or agreement about next steps. Instead, the conference was a symbolic victory: announcing common cause, if not common methods, among diverse people with differing viewpoints. The gathering's closing resolutions expressed satisfaction and optimism: "The Amenia Conference believes that its members have arrived at a virtual unanimity of opinion in regard to certain principles and that a more or less definite result may be expected from its deliberations." Historian August Meier describes those principles as "the desirability of all types of education, the importance of the ballot, and the necessity of replacing ancient suspicions and factions with respect for the good faith and methods of leaders in all parts of the country."[34]

James Weldon Johnson had enjoyed his experience at the Amenia gathering, where he had shared a tent and much conversation with W. E. B. Du Bois. But he was surprised when he received a letter from Joel Spingarn several months later asking him to consider an appointment as NAACP field secretary. "I had not received the slightest intimation of its likelihood," he later recalled. When the board of directors initially had decided to create the position of field secretary, Spingarn had contacted Morehouse College president John Hope about his possible interest in it. When Hope was not interested, Johnson seemed the perfect choice—someone who was viewed as more in the Booker T. Washington camp and could thereby demonstrate that unity for the cause would go well beyond the Amenia conference.[35] Additionally, Johnson's appointment addressed ongoing questions and arguments about the absence of Black people, other than Du Bois, in top-level NAACP executive positions. In late 1915, Joel had suggested to Mary White Ovington that he might consider resigning as board chair to allow for a Black successor. When association secretary May Childs Nerney resigned in 1916, she urged that her successor be a Black individual. Her work was greatly enlarged to create a new position that combined national organizing and fieldwork.[36]

Johnson began work in the New York office in December 1916 as the first NAACP field secretary and second full-time Black executive. His twofold agenda was to increase Black membership in the association and to expand the number of local branches, especially in the southern states, where there were only three branches—two in Louisiana and one in Key West, Florida.

Within two months, he took off on a speaking and mass meeting tour from Richmond, Virginia, to Tampa, Florida. He was convinced that the NAACP still needed to "awaken black America to a sense of its right and to a determination . . . to seek in every orderly way possible to secure all others to which it was entitled."[37] He sowed seeds of interest among Black people and concerned whites on his way south and then checked on their organizing efforts on his way back. His efforts in southern states soon netted more than 700 new members and 13 new branches in Virginia, North Carolina, South Carolina, Georgia, and Florida.[38]

The Spingarn brothers' father, Elias Spingarn, passed away at age 80 in December 1916. Survived by his wife and four sons, he left an estate estimated to be worth $228,156 ($6 million in 2022).[39] His tobacco business was initially represented by his son Harry. The other three (Arthur, Joel, and Sigmund) began to prepare for their part in the US involvement in the Great War.

CHAPTER EIGHT

Great War, Great Debates

As US participation in the war in Europe loomed, debate and excitement mounted. Soon to enter middle age and with limited interest in battles among foreign countries, both Arthur and Joel Spingarn might have been expected to adopt the pacifist leanings of many of their NAACP colleagues about the war. Mary White Ovington explained her antiwar views (shared with board members Oswald Garrison Villard, Lillian Wald, John Haynes Holmes, and others) as simply a lack of belief in the conflict—a sense that it was being "fought for purely imperialist motives and there was little to choose between English and German imperialism."[1] She particularly regretted that Joel's commitment to military ideals meant turning away from his "rare gift for teaching audacity and disobedience to forms."[2] For the Spingarn brothers, however, pacifism in the face of human suffering in Europe clashed with their sense of duty. Du Bois described Joel as "fired with consuming patriotism; he believed in America and feared Germany."[3]

Differences related to US participation in the Great War were only some of the varying attitudes afloat among individuals concerned with equality across race and color. As US involvement became certain, the idea of the draft began to raise additional opinions. Volunteer Black servicemen had long been limited almost exclusively to positions in labor battalions, mess tents, or other noncombat service and support areas. Their training was in units separate from those of white soldiers. Questions immediately arose about serving the cause of democracy in a situation of inequality and segregation. However, when white southerners in Congress spoke against drafting Black men, the NAACP lobbied for their inclusion as an example of fully participating citizenship. As one NAACP founder, Harry C. Smith, insisted: "The war, which every Afro-American looks upon as providential, will do much toward bettering our position, for it will again afford us an opportunity to show the metal of which we are made."[4] Much to the disappointment of most southern congressional leaders, the inclusive draft was initiated shortly after the United States entered World War I in April 1917. A single Black combat division, the 92nd, was also created.

Not surprisingly, Black conscripts faced differential treatment. They often were not given the same exemptions granted to white draftees, and they were sent to the least-favored training camps. Yet, in the issue of wartime service, even Du Bois seemed to cool his heated objections about disparities in the treatment of white and Black soldiers. In a controversial editorial in the *Crisis* that drew angry responses from many readers who had once supported his views, he exhorted Black citizens to "forget our special grievances and close our ranks shoulder to shoulder with our own white fellow citizens and the allied nations that are fighting for democracy." His stated rationale included: "That which the German power represents today spells death to the aspirations of Negroes and all darker races for equality, freedom and democracy."[5]

The dilemma that caused the most friction among NAACP members and staff related to the possibility of military officer training for Black men. Joel Spingarn realized that while this ideally would mean sending Black soldiers to training camps like the ones he had experienced at Plattsburgh and Fort Oglethorpe, those all-white installations would never agree to include Black trainees. To pursue his fight for trained Black officers meant supporting the development of segregated training camps, clearly a bitter pill for an individual in the forefront of the fight for equal access and equal rights. Convinced that Black officer training in an integrated setting would not happen, Joel insisted to the NAACP and others that the idea of a segregated training camp was his own and need not be viewed as an organizational project. In fact, the push for Black officer training, begun several months before US entry into the war, did reflect Joel's efforts in making contact with military decision-makers, writing letters, and issuing public statements. His personal certainty and commitment and his stubborn determination to act independently when necessary were reminiscent of his experience in taking on Columbia University leadership while many of his academic colleagues agreed only silently with his stance.

Early in 1917, Spingarn managed to secure a commitment for a Black officer training camp from the US Army commander, General Leonard Wood, on the condition that 200 satisfactory candidates could be quickly recruited.[6] As might be expected, the segregated camp proposal divided Black opinion. Spingarn insisted in a widely published open letter, addressed "To the educated colored men of the United States," that the four-week camp, while separate, would be the equal of white officer training and "conducted on exactly the same principle as the military training camp held at Plattsburg[h], N.Y., where thousands of men have received intensive training in military service." He also clarified that "men who are graduates or undergraduates of colleges, high schools, normal, agricultural or industrial schools, or other institutions of learning are preferred; but any man of intelligence, character and ability may join."[7]

Those who disagreed with developing segregated training camps, including many newspapers representing the growing Black press, quickly dubbed the effort as "Jim Crow camps." A stinging column in the *Chicago Defender* used that label in observing that "Dr. Spingarn is working to make such a camp a certainty by appealing to the more intelligent men." It then asserted that "he would have more hope of success if he attempted to secure results from the ignorant fellow who is incapable of discerning the harmful effect of accepting such restriction."[8] Strong objections also came from the *Baltimore Afro-American*, *Cleveland Gazette*, and *New York Age*, while supportive Black press included the *Washington Bee* and *Norfolk Journal*. Detractors typically pointed out that there were already Black army regiments with men who could be trained for officer positions serving in them. Even Black people who had known Spingarn as a friend and colleague, including Gilchrist Stewart and Archibald Grimké, worried that he was losing the confidence of others of their race. Others, such as retired first sergeant Charles R. Douglass, the son of famed abolitionist Frederick Douglass, publicly supported the proposed camp.[9]

Spingarn's open letter was particularly effective on the campuses of historically Black colleges, such as Howard University and Hampton Institute. By April 1917, the number of satisfactory applicants had exceeded General Wood's requisite 200. However, Wood's involvement in officer training had changed, causing some uncertainty about whether a training camp would happen. Spingarn developed a busy lobbying campaign in the US Congress and the War Department, while additional institutions, such as Fisk University and Morehouse College, yielded yet more applicants. By May, 470 Black men had applied for the training camp yet to be announced. At the same time, Joel took the lead in organizing the Amenia Home Guard in Dutchess County, enrolling 56 charter members for tasks needed to supply and conserve on the home front. He then left for his own officer training at Madison Barracks in upstate New York. Hopeful, but not entirely optimistic, about the reality of the Black officer training camp, he wrote to Howard University alumni secretary George William Cook: "I go with a heavy heart because I cannot share the opportunity with the hundreds of colored men who are more competent than I to take advantage of it."[10]

⚖

As if to publicly summarize his thoughts on literary criticism before the war swept him into full-time patriotic duty, Joel completed a book of essays, *Creative Criticism: Essays on the Unity of Genius and Taste*, which was published in 1917 by Henry Holt and Company. The small volume contained four essays on criticism in literature, drama, and verse, three of which had appeared earlier in other forms. In *Creative Criticism*, Spingarn reiterated his scholarly position that critique should emphasize literary creators and their success in meeting personal aims, rather than any success in predetermined measures of style and uses of devices like metaphor, simile, and theme. In a highly favorable article, a *New York Times* reviewer noted: "in thus simplifying the critic's work, freeing it from its old-time technicalities, he has brought it closer to popular needs and comprehension. . . . This 'unity of genius and taste' is a central element in Professor Spingarn's theory."[11] Even some of his earlier academic doubters now supported his approach. Undoubtedly very pleasing to Spingarn was the response of H. L. Mencken, who singled him out as "one of the few campus critics worth listening to."[12]

NAACP board members were initially uncertain about whether to replace Joel as their chair during his military commitments or to have him retain his title while naming an "assistant chairman"—most likely Mary White Ovington—to carry out his duties. NAACP secretary Roy Nash wrote to Joel describing the board's concern that Spingarn would not want to be viewed as part of the NAACP criticism of US government actions while he was serving as a US Army officer. "The NAACP must remain in a position where it can frankly criticize the government," Nash insisted, explaining that the organization already planned to draw attention to "the deadly parallel between our enemy abroad and the enemy in the South."[13] Ultimately, Joel's NAACP duties were placed with Ovington as acting board chair, and the board soon officially endorsed the idea of a separate Black officer training camp. Du Bois, still somewhat unexpectedly supportive of the segregated officer training, concluded in a column in the *Crisis*: "We must choose then between the insult of a separate camp and the irreparable injury of strengthening the present custom of putting no black men in positions of authority. . . . We did not make the damnable dilemma. Our enemies made that."[14]

James Weldon Johnson, acting in the executive secretary position at the NAACP, continued to put pressure on the military bureaucracy for the training camp after Spingarn's departure for Madison Barracks. During the last week of May, Johnson was informed that a segregated officer training camp had been secured at Fort Des Moines, Iowa, and it would begin on June 18 under the command of Brigadier General Charles C. Ballou. By mid-October 1917, officer commissions from the camp included 106 captains, 329 first lieutenants, and 204 second lieutenants. Additional commissions followed.[15] The Fort Des Moines training camp closed shortly after.

Black draftees and volunteers generally experienced no equal treatment with white soldiers. Historian David M. Kennedy observes: "Only one in every five black men sent to France saw combat, while in the [American Expeditionary Forces] as a whole two out of three soldiers took part in battle." Instead, "they worked as stevedores in the Atlantic ports and [as] common laborers at camps in the Services of the Rear in France."[16] However, some Black soldiers did take on new and coveted duties as guards of prominent people and of places key to the war effort. These assignments were prompted by worries that German spies and double agents might be lurking anywhere but were highly unlikely to have dark skin. James Weldon Johnson noted on a 1917 visit to Washington, DC, that "every man of the troops guarding the home of the President and the offices of the three principal departments of the government was a black man."[17]

But for Black trainees in camps that placed them in segregated units within white regiments, particularly in the South, racial tension seemed to expand in the military installations and nearby communities. Langston Hughes, cataloging wartime discrimination, found that Black soldiers were barred from white religious services at Camp Lee in Virginia and from the YMCA at Camp Greene in North Carolina. Mob action near training camps and beyond resulted in 20 more lynchings in 1918 than in the previous year. The humiliation of Jim Crow segregation grew, as did skirmishes in the streets when whites confronted Black soldiers. A riot involving an all-Black regiment in Houston resulted in the deaths of more than 20 Black and white citizens.

The NAACP staffs in New York and in local branches had their hands full with investigations of increasing discriminatory treatment. Walter White, a graduate of Atlanta University, was hired as assistant secretary in 1918. A mixed-heritage Black man with light skin and blue eyes, he could often pass for white to get valuable information in investigations of lynchings and other racial injustices throughout the South.[18]

𝄢

Joel and Arthur Spingarn both took leaves of absence from their NAACP positions to serve their country during the Great War, but in very different capacities. Joel trained to eventually serve as an army major. Arthur's expertise in the spread and control of social diseases launched his service in the Sanitary Corps, a division of the US Army Medical Department headed by the surgeon general in Washington, DC. The corps commissioned officers "with special skills in sanitation, sanitary engineering, bacteriology, or other sciences related to sanitation and preventive medicine, or who possess other knowledge of special advantage to the Medical Department."[19] Arthur's work in the nation's capital gave him up-close experiences with the racism in US government offices. He later related a telling example:

> They segregated all negro stenographers. There was one stenographer, very light, who kept avoiding me. One night, after everyone had gone home, I called her over. I said, "I know your family. I'm not going to say anything." She passed, you see. She got a bigger salary and was very much better off. Otherwise, she would have to be in the cellar. This was in the first war. All negroes were segregated and in the cellar.[20]

Arthur's knowledge of sanitation and hygiene allowed him to speak, write, and advise concerning social disease prevention and treatment—largely venereal disease and largely among Black soldiers. As an army captain, he was assigned to the Social Hygiene Division of the Commission on Training Camp Activities (CTCA), where he served as assistant director. CTCA was concerned with troop morale, as well as morals. One of his early endeavors was to coauthor a booklet titled *Keeping Fit to Fight*. However, he noted that, primarily due to illustrations depicting white soldiers, it was "no good for negro soldiers." He convinced his superiors to let him write a new version to be distributed to Black troops.[21]

Early in 1918, Arthur embarked on a lengthy tour "to investigate conditions influencing the prevalence of venereal diseases among the colored troops and conditions favoring infection of white troops by colored women in civilian communities accessible to military forces." That work took him to training camps in Virginia, North Carolina, South Carolina, Georgia, Alabama, Tennessee, Kentucky, and Ohio.[22] In Birmingham, Alabama, he gained firsthand understanding of the challenges confronting trainees. Upon arrival, he found himself on foot at night walking three blocks to his hotel from the railway station, not far from the camp he was to inspect. "I was solicited by four or five women and three or four bootleggers," he recalled. This eye-opening experience was quite different from various earlier camp inspections, when local officials had toured him around by car. Especially concerned about the health of Black recruits, he frequently pushed for their treatment by reminding decision-makers that "the incidence of venereal disease is greater among negro troops than among white," and "practically all these troops had contracted these infections prior to their induction into the Army."[23]

At various camps, Arthur not only investigated and reported, but also pitched in to start clubs and societies that would promote hygiene and healthy on-site recreational activities. He helped organize and incorporate the Circle for Negro War Relief in 1917 "to furnish aid and assistance to Negroes and their families while preparing for and while in the military service." Later, the organization emphasized public health in Black communities, and Arthur served on its board of directors until 1921.[24]

While he was happy to be back after weeks of travel to various camps, he wrote to Amy Spingarn at Troutbeck that he had suffered a slight bout of the 1918 influenza. In Washington, he found the pandemic "much worse than in New York; about ninety deaths a day with a total of over a thousand fatalities so far. All conductors, elevator girls, barbers, etc. go about masked."[25]

After Arthur Spingarn's appointment in the Sanitary Corps, the NAACP legal program retreated from proactively searching out test cases and switched to monitoring various legal developments and rulings related to racial prejudice and injustice, including many involving the treatment of Black soldiers. Charles Studin replaced Spingarn as chair of the legal committee. In early 1918, at age 39, Arthur Spingarn was married in Washington, DC, to Marion Mayer Goldman, a social worker he had known for some time. She had been the director of investigation for the New York Probation and Protective Association, and shortly after moving to Washington, she was put in charge of a newly established women's bureau in the District of Columbia Police Department. The department gave her the title "director of women's work" and the rank of detective sergeant, announcing that the 20 or so women reporting to her would be limited to detective work—and only until men returned from their wartime duties.[26]

Joel's health had been compromised by various past illnesses related to a duodenal ulcer. However, he stretched his physical limitations in order to succeed in military training. When he managed to graduate from officer training with the rank of major in the infantry, he was one of only 3 of more than 2,000 men at Madison Barracks to do so. In the summer of 1917, he was assigned the command of a battalion at the newly constructed Camp Dix in New Jersey. Only Mary White Ovington was disappointed for him, writing that he was compromising his independence to join "a path ruled by authority."[27]

After the completion of weeks of training, Major Spingarn was thrilled to leave the camp with his battalion to prepare for departure to France, where his younger brother Sigmund was already serving as an army captain. However, Joel fell ill with severe ulcer pain before reaching the port of embarkation. He was granted a lengthy leave of absence and had a surgery that cut into his stomach, removed the duodenum, and reconnected portions of the intestine.[28] During his convalescence in New Jersey and Manhattan, he forwarded to Arthur any correspondence that concerned his NAACP or literary activities. "I haven't the energy to read and comment," he wrote to his brother concerning a packet of poems sent to him in November 1917.[29]

Yet another great setback was on the horizon. In mid-December, Joel's beloved home at Troutbeck was engulfed by a fire of unknown cause, which started in the attic while only a caretaker was present. Firefighters from the town of Amenia were delayed by deep snow, and the home suffered damages estimated at $150,000 ($3.3 million in 2022).[30]

Disappointment piled on disappointment as Spingarn was released from sick leave but, although feeling at least somewhat recovered, still was not permitted to join his battalion in France. Instead, early in 1918, he was assigned to the Intelligence Branch of the Army General Staff in Washington, DC. Although he remained hopeful of eventually joining the action overseas, he also was determined to make his stateside desk job more than just routine. He set out to create an Intelligence Branch program of "constructive measures" for Black people by "redressing the grievances which beset Negroes during the war and encouraging Negroes' loyalty and patriotism rather than merely attempting to censure and uncover disloyalty."[31] He was well aware that the program he proposed—requiring military intelligence to commission Black military officers—was "contrary to all the traditions and deepest instincts of the officers of the General Staff." He reasoned that although his vocal and persistent push for such a program "roused the enmity of all the powers that be," it also supported his eventual goal to leave Washington for an overseas assignment. "If I became a persona non grata, I might be sent elsewhere; might even be sent to the front."[32]

Spingarn did manage to convince his superiors to consider a captain's commission for W. E. B. Du Bois, who would then join the General Staff in his area and take charge of a new bureau with initiatives related to Black soldiers. Du Bois was formally approached in mid-June about his willingness to accept such a position if it were to be established. He agreed on the condition that he could continue to edit the *Crisis* and direct the Department of Publications and Research, drawing his NAACP salary, minus any needed for additional editorial assistance, to supplement his military pay. After all, he reasoned, he had a family to support and uncertain postwar prospects if he were to leave his NAACP employment.

At the July NAACP board meeting, his colleagues recognized his potential contribution to the country, but questioned if he should retain his *Crisis* editorship and Department of Publications and Research directorship. Arthur Spingarn, serving in Washington, DC, but still a member of the board of directors, wrote in support of Du Bois's proposal to serve as a captain in the Intelligence Branch while maintaining his NAACP position. However, the majority of the board voted against those terms. Joel had pushed Du Bois to consider the captaincy and assured him that a break in his NAACP employment would not be permanent. Then, dismayed at the board's stance and its discouraging effect on Du Bois's enthusiasm for the army commission, he resigned as board chair. Clearly, this did not change the immediate workings of the organization, since Ovington had been acting as chair, but it sent a message about Joel's reaction to adverse internal decisions. Shortly, the issue was taken out of the hands of those who had been most involved. Du Bois explained the closure of the matter: "The General Staff . . . decided not to establish the proposed bureau at present, as its broad scope might lead 'beyond the proper bounds of military activity.' "[33]

⚖

Joel worked at his intelligence post only about 10 weeks. Shortly after the demise of his idea for a new unit headed by Du Bois, he got permission to leave for duty overseas as a battalion commander. He was sent to the Alsace-Lorraine region of northern France, which had experienced numerous battles between nearby German armies and Allied troops. Not long after arriving and a month prior to the armistice, he wrote to Du Bois about his sense of both pride and loss:

> The ties of home assume a new meaning to us here in France, and when the
> guns rumble, as they do continuously not far off, *The Crisis* and the many

friends whom it brings to mind seem very near and dear. . . . The other day
I made Sunday afternoon a holiday and paid my first visit to the largest city in
this section [Nancy] . . . the sorely tried city in a semi-circle of the hills which it
in part climbed. It had been bombed and bombarded for years, and a large part
of the civil population was evacuated last winter. Everywhere I saw signs of
sufferings.

I sought out the Faculty of Letters (it is a University city). But I found only
the old concierge, who told me there had been no professors, students, or studies since the city was evacuated. She showed me the great hall of the University, and I mounted the rostrum and made my first address in French. My only
audience was the concierge, who complimented me on my eloquence. . . . But
though my French was really very bad, and the audience limited, I delivered
my message. . . . I began with the thought that one could love France very
dearly without speaking perfect French, just as one could love God without
speaking the language of angels. I ended by tipping my audience and leaving
the University. At the corner I bought a paper, and this startling headline
stared me in the face: *L'Ennemi demande l'armistice.*[34]

Joel also wrote frequently to his mother, to Amy, and to his eldest daughter, Hope, and they in turn read his letters to the younger three children. He
encouraged their schoolwork and advised about their manners and duties.
And he often included souvenirs of foreign money, French and German writing paper, and newspaper items.[35] In a later autobiographical fragment, he
recalled some of his most vivid memories: "I smelt gunpowder. I had the
taste of both defensive and offensive warfare. I talked to German soldiers on
the other side of No Man's Land within hours after the Armistice. I was the
first American officer in several German towns."[36]

Joel's presence at the field of battle sharpened Arthur's frustration at
being in far less action at home. "I cannot tell you how much I envy you the
experience," he wrote to Joel. While Arthur insisted that he had no bitterness
about his domestic assignment, he noted that "there is probably not a single
man I know in Washington who would not gladly have made any sacrifice for
a chance to get over." Although Arthur and all other men in his section had
requested overseas service, only one had been assigned abroad. He admitted
to Joel, "I cannot deny a keen sense of disappointment. . . . The feeling that I
am needed has not made it any easier to stay here, but I have to content myself with little field trips."[37]

⚖

Observing Black soldiers in France, Joel reported that "colored America has more than justified the hopes of those who have always believed in it." However, most Black men serving in the army were assigned to labor, not combat, battalions. They were not in the marines, and they served largely as cooks and mess staff in the navy. Ovington recalled Joel speaking of "white officers who deliberately failed to give the colored division the training that was right." He saw those military leaders as "traitors in that they preferred to lose a battle to seeing the colored officer return home distinguished, honored."[38]

Ovington later reported on the discriminatory conditions that followed Black troops overseas, where they were generally "a center of controversy" among white soldiers and a curiosity among villagers in France. She noted that although "a French hotel would welcome a Negro, a white officer would order him out." French reporter Jean Boileau wrote in a *Baltimore Evening Sun* article of the wartime interactions between Black Americans and French citizens: "Many French girls received more courtesy and better treatment from the American Negroes than from the whites. No Negro ever referred to a French woman as a 'jane' or any other epithet. I notice that even your correspondent uses the term 'frog jane' in reference to the French girl."[39]

Arthur's service finally did take him to France in early 1919, shortly after the November 1918 armistice, to inspect and advise about conditions in military rest camps, where soldiers awaited passage home. Stationed in Chambéry in southeastern France, he also spent time in Brest, Tours, and Beaune. His only remaining disappointment was that he did not get a chance to meet up with Joel when both were in France. However, he managed several visits with their brother Sigmund, who was in an American hospital in Lyon recovering from "a mild case of typhoid."[40]

Joel remained in France for four months beyond the armistice. He served under Brigadier General William Westervelt as a member of a commission studying artillery types, sizes, and transport in order to recommend guidelines for future military readiness. His NAACP colleague W. E. B. Du Bois headed to France during the Paris Peace Conference, which hammered out the Treaty of Versailles. There, in February 1919 he helped to organize the first Pan-African Congress, aimed at assuring that African countries and colonies, as well as island nations, would move toward self-governance and could reap economic and social benefits for their own citizens. Fifty-seven delegates attended from the United States, the West Indies, Africa, and Europe. Joel provided introductions that helped connect Du Bois with influential friends in Paris, including noted historian George Beer, who was serving as a member and as African advisor on the American Commission to Negotiate Peace. Spingarn then addressed the Pan-African Congress in Paris before he left for New York.[41]

According to Du Bois, "The results of this Pan-African meeting were small, but it had some influence." Delegates sent several resolutions to the peace conference and set the stage for more such Pan-African meetings. Additionally, the NAACP board of directors had asked Du Bois to investigate the treatment and accomplishments of Black soldiers in France. When he heard of the soldiers' experiences, he recalled, "I became convinced and said that American white officers fought more valiantly against Negroes than they did against the Germans."[42]

CHAPTER NINE

Aftermath

Arthur Spingarn arrived in Atlanta, Georgia, in May 1920 for his first NAACP national conference since his wartime service. He departed the train that had carried him south with his colleague James Weldon Johnson. Not surprisingly, they immediately caught stares as a mixed-race duo walking and chatting together through the Atlanta station. Johnson later recalled that a Red Cap porter had picked up their bags on the platform, carrying one in each hand. But he walked slowly and haltingly as he tried to decide "whether to break the laws of Georgia by taking the white man through the Jim Crow exit with me, or by taking me through the white folks' exit [the main station entrance] with him." After several hesitations, the porter "showed real courage and successfully risked the chance of taking us both through the main entrance."[1]

The Atlanta conference, with more than 200 NAACP delegates and 3,000 attendees at nightly public sessions, was viewed by NAACP leadership as an announcement of the organization's nationwide presence, even in the South.[2] It also allowed many northern delegates to observe the current southern culture and behavior firsthand. Arthur Spingarn had returned from Washington, DC, and France to his NAACP position as chair of the organization's legal committee, providing oversight and strategy regarding legal efforts at the national level. At the Atlanta conference, he was the keynote speaker at the first national civil rights meeting to be held in the South. Substituting for the organization's ailing president, Moorfield Storey, Spingarn maintained the matter-of-fact tone, neither conciliatory nor challenging, that had long marked his communication style: "We have no views to present that are so radical that they cannot be found in the Sermon on the Mount or in the

Constitution of the United States. Mutual tolerance, mutual sympathy, and mutual respect must be cultivated. All our problems must be solved with justice."[3]

The conference came on the heels of a world war and postwar changes that affected the NAACP and the country. Jobs in the North prompted a renewed migration of southern Black citizens to cities like St. Louis, Chicago, Cleveland, and Detroit. By one account, "the Pennsylvania Railroad alone drew 10,000 black workers out of Florida and South Georgia."[4] Those who stayed in the South, however, faced growing inequalities and injustices.

During the wartime preparation and involvement, with James Weldon Johnson serving as NAACP field secretary and acting executive secretary and Mary White Ovington acting as board chair, Walter White had traveled throughout the South to investigate lynchings, mob violence, and race riots. Ovington and W. E. B. Du Bois had barely managed to keep the national office afloat. Finally, in the spring of 1918, NAACP pioneering founder and board member Oswald Garrison Villard had taken the lead in hiring an experienced white businessman, John Shillady, as executive secretary. Ovington later described Shillady as competent, prepared, and ready to produce change. Shillady started an ambitious program to raise paid memberships from 10,000 to 50,000, hired the necessary clerks, moved the office to a larger space, and worked to increase funding for specific campaigns. The first and foremost of these was the antilynching effort.[5]

Shillady called for a review and overhaul of the NAACP's lynching case materials. In 1919, geographical statistics, victim data, the absence of prosecutions, and key case findings were compiled in an NAACP book, *Thirty Years of Lynching in the United States, 1889–1918*. It covered a time period when 3,224 lynchings had occurred, primarily killing Black men, largely by public burning or hanging.[6] The Dyer Anti-Lynching Bill, introduced in Congress by Missouri representative Leonidas Dyer in 1918, sought to make lynching a federal crime. The NAACP began extensive lobbying for its passage. Arthur Spingarn, a longtime advocate for action against lynching, explained what studies of the situation had uncovered:

> The fiction that the South created was that this was to protect white womanhood and that the negroes were raping white women. Well, the actual facts were that not even five percent of those lynched were even accused of attacking white women. People were lynched for unbelievable reasons—for owning automobiles better than white people, or because they were uppity and putting

on airs. One was lynched because he called a woman "Mrs." He should call her "Miss Alice" or "Miss Mary." And the brutality was just unconceivable.[7]

Spingarn was happy to testify in early 1920 before the US House Judiciary Committee, insisting that "the government must find some means of stamping out lynchings. . . . If it is not possible under the Constitution, then the Constitution should be amended." Although there were 55 additional lynchings that year, following 58 in 1918 and 70 in 1919, the reintroduced Dyer bill, which was accompanied by extensive public pressure and organized lobbying, provided some glimmer of optimism. It finally was passed by the US House of Representatives in January 1922, but it headed to a Senate in the grip of a powerful bloc of southern conservatives. The NAACP ran a full-page ad in major newspapers headlined "The Shame of America," which noted the United States as the only country where human beings were being burned at the stake. Nevertheless, conservative southern senators managed to halt the passage of the Dyer bill.[8]

Postwar racial unrest soon grew to rioting, often in places where Black workers were beginning to organize and demand an end to peonage and other discriminatory treatment. Du Bois had warned at the war's end: "We return. We return from fighting. We return fighting." The year 1919 saw race riots in several southern states, including Arkansas and Texas, but also in Illinois and Nebraska—26 race riots in all. Ovington observed the postwar realities: "It was a disquieting summer. Negro soldiers were coming home and some were in no mood to return to their former position. There were many clashes." The clash most immediately relevant to the NAACP happened when the new executive secretary, Shillady, went to Austin, Texas, to speak with state officials about issues concerning local branches. There, he was attacked and beaten outside his hotel by a small mob, including a local constable and county judge. Fortunately, he managed to get on a train back to New York. With waning confidence in what the NAACP could accomplish against such vitriolic opposition, he resigned his position within a year.[9]

⚖️

Joel Spingarn had returned from France proud to have served, but weary in spirit and somewhat precarious in health. However, he did manage a western US trip in the summer of 1919 to renew his familiarity with issues and activities nationwide. He motored through the city of Chicago with poet Carl Sandburg, particularly taking in the South Side area torn apart by race rioting a month earlier. He then met with Illinois governor Frank Lowden. From there, he and Amy traveled by train on a vacation tour of New Mexico that included hiking, camping, and visiting Indigenous pueblos, canyons, and ancient cliff dwellings.[10] He reluctantly accepted the very part-time role of NAACP treasurer, but only on the condition that he would not undertake fundraising. He also served as chair of the *Crisis* committee and returned as a member of the board of directors.

With an ongoing stream of relapses and recoveries related to his continuing ulcer problems, Joel was most comfortable at Troutbeck with his family, friendly visitors, gardening projects, community involvement, scholarly writing, and scenic vistas. His and Amy's four children now ranged in age from 7 years old to 13. He maintained his Upper East Side townhome in Manhattan. However, he saw less of Arthur than before the war and rarely attended NAACP board meetings. Biographer B. Joyce Ross concludes that, particularly in northern cities, a growing Black identification and determination, combined with the intellectual and artistic spirit of the Harlem Renaissance, had "rendered obsolete Spingarn's brand of personal activism."[11] Additionally, the administrative maturation of the NAACP—by 1920 it had a strong core of paid staff and more than 300 branches—meant that it was poised to move from a young, goal-directed organization to a socially essential institution.

Observing the new climate, Joel wrote to James Weldon Johnson that "a great change has come over the men and women of Negro descent throughout the country." He hoped it would soon alleviate the problem of "a large minority who are willing to admit their eternal inferiority and serfdom."[12] His views concerning the evolving struggle for racial equality, as well as his need to improve his physical health after the strain of war, undoubtedly helped to prompt Joel's decision to place his professional interests largely on literary projects. The most prominent of these began when two 1904 Columbia graduates, Alfred Harcourt and Donald C. Brace, resigned from their positions at Henry Holt and Company in 1919 to start their own publishing house. Determined to be relevant to trends in both Europe and the United States, they quickly approached Joel. He became the general editor of a Harcourt, Brace and Company division called the European Library, which sought to expand Americans' understanding of European ideas and influence in thought and literature. In his new role, Joel was able to encourage the publication of works by authors of French, Italian, German, Austrian, and other European nationalities. The timing of the new venture was perfect for fulfilling his renewed literary concerns well beyond issues of criticism. It fit well with his growing interest in intellectual and artistic links between Europe

Joel Spingarn at Troutbeck. Photograph by Carl Van Vechten, Yale Collection of American Literature, Beinecke Rare Book and Manuscript Library; used with permission of the Van Vechten Trust

and the United States. During this time, he also published essays in the *Free-man*, the *Nation*, and the *Dial*. His edited anthology published by Harcourt, Brace, *Criticism in America: Its Function and Status*, included essays by H. L. Mencken, Irving Babbitt, Van Wyck Brooks, T. S. Eliot, and other literary luminaries of the day.[13] However, surgery in 1922 and subsequent poor health slowed Joel's literary activity and prompted his transfer to off-site duty at Harcourt, Brace in 1924.

☒☒

A changing of the guard at the NAACP further marked the differences of the postwar era. After three years of leadership and political diplomacy in establishing branches and building the association, James Weldon Johnson was appointed in November 1920 as the first Black executive secretary. Walter White was named assistant executive secretary, and William Pickens stepped into the field secretary role. Of the seven top full-time staff members, only the newly appointed press officer, Herbert Seligman, was white.[14] However, this trend in the NAACP staff's racial composition did not extend to the legal work. Arthur Spingarn, one of five NAACP vice presidents and once again chair of the national legal committee, was assisted by Walter White. Cases taking place in the branches were most often handled by white attorneys, as were the cases working their way toward the Supreme Court. Legal historians Meier and Rudwick point out that even NAACP Black leaders in the immediate postwar years favored white attorneys, likely due to "problems besetting the black legal profession and the NAACP's ability to secure the services of certain highly distinguished white attorneys."[15] Among the most notable of those during the 1920s were the aging Moorfield Storey, Louis Marshall, and Clarence Darrow.

In addition to his legal committee work, Arthur was among those at the NAACP who pushed the idea that the organization should investigate and ultimately seek to end the US occupation and financial control of Haiti. Seligman and Johnson made trips to Haiti in 1920 to examine the racial discrimination that had resulted from martial law under US Marine forces since 1915. Numerous NAACP approaches to the Woodrow Wilson administration prior to US involvement in World War I had not resulted in any commitments to improve the treatment of Haitian Black citizens. Du Bois insisted that "Haiti stood with Liberia as a continuing symbol of Negro revolt against slavery and oppression, and capacity for self-rule." In the *Crisis*, he frequently publicized the "exploitation at the hands of New York City banks and plundering speculators," which had led to US imperialism over the Black country.

When Arthur Spingarn visited Haiti in 1923, he became friendly with a number of Haitian academic and diplomatic leaders, such as poet and lawyer Georges Sylvain. Spingarn determined that the NAACP should push the US government to return Haiti to the Haitians. Soon after, Oswald Garrison Villard invited him to join a group he was forming to expose the "rampant American imperialism" in Haiti and to lobby Congress and the Calvin Coolidge administration for "action consistent with the best American traditions and consonant with the obvious needs for world peace."[16] Yet the US occupation lasted until 1934.

Also drawing Spingarn into NAACP concerns beyond his legal activities was the ongoing effort to increase contributions from large donors. As historian Hasia Diner observes, "Arthur Spingarn, for one, often served as an intermediary between the NAACP and wealthy Jews and was always conscious of the potential for even more Jewish support. . . . When he compiled names of possible NAACP donors in 1920, nineteen of his thirty-five people were Jews." Walter White periodically checked with Spingarn about whom to approach among potential Jewish donors, asking for his opinion on wording in fundraising letters.[17]

Notable Jewish men like Julius Rosenwald, Jacob Schiff, Herbert Lehman, and Felix Warburg were able and willing to support good causes, including equal rights for Black citizens. A tradition of philanthropy with theological roots in Europe had continued with Jewish immigration to the United States. Citing riots, lynchings, and anti-immigrant sentiments following World War I, David Levering Lewis concludes, "By the early 1920s, assimilationist Jews and integrationist Afro-Americans needed each other more than ever."[18] W. E. B. Du Bois had emphasized the idea of a kinship among Black and Jewish communities in early *Crisis* editorials. For example, he wrote that with the 1916 Supreme Court nomination of Louis Brandeis, "we have a man who, as a Jew, knows what it is to be despised and rejected of men . . . and what the curse of poverty means and what its abolition involves." Discussing the shared experiences of bias in a later *Crisis*, he excoriated Yale, Harvard, and Columbia Universities for their renewed and very open commitments to "get rid of Jews in the University as far as possible, both from the faculty and from the student body." He continued that this "strikes the Negro as curiously paradoxical. The Negro has been objected to apparently for lack of brains and for low culture; the Jew is now objected to for excess of brains and over-keen mentality. All the world fears this group of thinkers."[19]

⚖

As chair of the NAACP legal committee, Arthur preferred to work largely behind the scenes, examining issues of discrimination and injustice for possible NAACP legal involvement, determining which of many worthy cases to pursue, and advising NAACP branch and outside attorneys. "It's always been my practice to keep in the background," he insisted. However, according to a study of NAACP legal activities through the years, he "came to play a more crucial role than any other Board member, white or black. Given the salience of the legal program, the legal committee chairman was a central figure." Yet Spingarn rarely offered advice to other lawyers charged with handling cases, instead "functioning as a 'wise counselor' who assisted only when asked."[20] His calm and considered demeaner also marked him as a kindly friend, supporting colleagues beyond the scope of his legal work. For example, Du Bois was surprised and hurt when organizers of the 1923 NAACP national conference in Kansas City failed to put him on the program. Rather than appeal to the group, he later sought solace by simply sharing his feelings with Arthur.[21]

One case that did draw Arthur into the spotlight of the US Supreme Court was a voting rights issue in Texas. A 1923 state law banned Black Democrats from voting in their party's primaries, which, given the state's conservative strength, generally foretold the ultimate election results. When Lawrence A. Nixon, a local Black physician and El Paso NAACP branch member, sued after being turned away at the polls in the Democratic Party primary, the Texas lower courts dismissed his case. The NAACP appealed to the US Supreme Court and hired a Texas attorney to plead the case, *Nixon v. Herndon*. Spingarn had written briefs and planned the approach.

Much to Spingarn's surprise, during a courtroom recess, the Texan felt overwhelmed and asked Spingarn to please take over the remainder of the oral argument. Although Chief Justice William Taft initially objected to the sudden switch, he finally agreed. But "I wasn't ready to argue for two hours without preparation," recalled Spingarn. Nevertheless, he stood tall, took deep breaths, and tried to draw on what he recalled from the written briefs. Then, he later wrote, he simply "put in a lot of hot air." He was encouraged, however, when "Judge Brandeis winked at me. . . . He knew what was happening. I had exhausted all the law I could think of in about an hour and a half."[22] Fortunately, the attorney general of Texas made a last-minute request to file a brief, allowing for a reargument of the case several weeks later. The NAACP called on a new legal committee member, the eminent civil rights and constitutional lawyer Louis Marshall, to develop the reply brief. The unanimous Supreme Court decision, handed down in March 1927, reversed the lower court rulings and said the law was in violation of nondiscrimination guarantees in the Fourteenth Amendment.

Over the next 15 years, the state of Texas continued to test various methods of Black voter suppression. One of these, a state statute giving political parties their own choice in determining qualified voters, also made its way to the Supreme Court in 1932 as *Nixon v. Condon*. The statute was successfully argued down by Spingarn, and it was overturned in a 5–4 decision. Perhaps inevitably, after failing to reserve primary voting for white citizens only, the Texas Democratic Party then barred Black voters from participating in its nominating conventions.

Spingarn was careful to include Black lawyers from local branches whenever possible in cases headed to court with NAACP support. And he was happy when they stood front and center in courtrooms to contribute both their legal abilities and their community knowledge. However, he often found it difficult to either find or interest the right local lawyers. James Cobb, for example, was a highly regarded Black lawyer who headed legal activities of the Washington, DC, branch. He brought a residential housing discrimination issue to the attention of the national office and was instrumental in taking it to the Supreme Court in 1926 as *Corrigan v. Buckley*. Restrictive neighborhood covenants were increasingly used as end runs around the decision against racial discrimination reached in *Buchanan v. Warley*. When Irene Corrigan ignored a racially restrictive covenant by selling her Washington, DC, house to a Black couple, Cobb approached Spingarn and Johnson for NAACP assistance. After losses in the lower courts, the Supreme Court agreed to take the case. Cobb, however, may have seen insurmountable difficulties with the case or he may have worried about his own chance of success. He volunteered to Spingarn that other lawyers might be better suited for the final chapter, writing that "no especial pride is to be mine in arguing the case before the Supreme Court. I shall be happy to have Messrs. Marshall and Davis, or Mr. Storey, if you please, present it."[23] Ultimately, Louis Marshall made the oral argument. However, the Supreme Court upheld the lower courts' dismissal of the case, finding no constitutional basis for a ruling.

⚖

The issue of using prominent white or local Black attorneys met with little time or opportunity for debate when word reached James Weldon Johnson and Arthur Spingarn of a racially charged disturbance and shooting in Detroit in September 1925. Ossian Sweet was a noted Black physician who had graduated from Howard University Medical School before moving to Detroit in 1921. He had just returned to the city with his wife, Gladys, after a year of additional medical study in France. They purchased a small house that had been owned by a mixed-race couple in a white, middle-class neighborhood. But community members had watched as migrating southern Black people swelled in number in Detroit from 8,000 to 65,000 in a dozen years. They were ready to fight for the kind of neighborhood they preferred.

The Sweets saw early signs of trouble and asked friends and family to join them at their new house when they moved in. On their second night in residence, a mob of hundreds pelted their home with rocks, which smashed windows and dented shutters. Police arrived but did not try to disperse the crowd or stop the violence. Finally, a single shot was fired by one of the 11 people inside the home. It struck and killed a man in the crowd, and those in the Sweets' home were taken into custody without bail. Spingarn and Johnson sent Walter White to investigate, and he immediately took control by arriving at the jail and getting the defendants to formally assign representation to the NAACP.[24]

While local branch leaders and various members of Detroit's Black community lobbied for local, preferably Black, lawyers to handle the case, White determined that only the very best white lawyers would have a chance. Finally, amid grumbling from white and Black branch members, Spingarn and White wrote a joint memo warning that if the NAACP could not fully determine the best attorneys to retain, it would back out of the case.[25] Those attorneys turned out to be the heroic lawyer of the recent Scopes trial, Clarence Darrow, and his Dayton-based assistant litigator, Arthur Garfield Hays.

Spingarn and White first met Darrow at Hays's New York City home. They brought with them, perhaps for dramatic effect, NAACP executive secretary James Weldon Johnson and Charles Studin, assistant chair of the legal committee. Spingarn recounted for Darrow the sad events of racial hatred that had unfolded at the Sweets' new home, including the deadly rifle shot from Sweet's younger brother Henry. Darrow, who had just met the four NAACP leaders for the first time, seemed genuinely sympathetic. He leaned toward Spingarn and in almost a whisper said, "I understand. I know the suffering your people have endured." Always somewhat swarthy, Spingarn had added more color while outdoors on summer weekends. He quickly informed Darrow that "I don't happen to be a Negro." The surprise for Darrow continued when blue-eyed, light-skinned Walter White told him that he indeed was "colored."[26] Darrow consented to take the case for $5,000, which was far less than his usual fee. The NAACP managed to raise the funds to defend the 11 men in the house that night, who were being tried together for conspiracy to murder.

Spingarn and White spent a great deal of time in Detroit throughout the fall and into the spring. When *People v. Sweet* began at trial in Detroit in late October 1925, it commanded great attention among Black citizens throughout the country. Walter White had called it a case "bigger than Detroit or Michigan . . . a dramatic climax of the nationwide fight to enforce residential segregation."[27] The jury, 12 white men, deadlocked, and Judge Frank Murphy declared a mistrial. The second trial, with a new group of white male jurors, began in late April 1926. Clarence Darrow pulled no punches about the mob racism of the white citizens outside the Sweet residence. James Weldon Johnson later described with awe Darrow's six-hour final argument:

> At times his voice was low as though he was coaxing a child. . . . At other times, his words came like flashes of lightning and crashes of thunder. He closed his argument with a plea that left no eyes dry. When he finished, I walked over to him to express my appreciation and thanks. . . . I tried to stammer out a few words, but broke down and wept.[28]

The jury verdict of not guilty was celebrated far and wide, with proponents of racial justice happily supporting the conclusion of the Baltimore newspaper the *Afro-American*: "If the National Association [NAACP] had done nothing else but win the day in the Sweet segregation case, its years of activity and thousands of dollars it has spent have justified its existence."[29]

⚖

Joel Spingarn continued to battle recurring health problems, largely due to the formation of new ulcers. Within a few years of his return from wartime duties, he reported that "about a third of the time has been spent in bed with pain, inability to eat food, mental depression, etc."[30] He remained mostly at his Amenia estate, but spent the winter in New York City. His activities with the NAACP were largely through letters and occasional meetings. When Walter White decided to pursue his writing by accepting a three-year Guggenheim Fellowship in France, Joel stepped into the forefront of efforts to keep White at the NAACP. Inviting White to his Manhattan townhouse on West 72nd Street, he expressed his disappointment that White would "give up what I had thought was to be your life work." In what turned out to be an unusual conversation, he grilled the light-skinned White on his feelings toward full versus mixed-blood "negroes." In a letter to Amy, he recalled that White "admitted he had virtually never met a pure Negro whom he really could trust. . . . they were inferior." For Joel, this indicated a widespread conundrum: "The passionate pro-Negro loyalty is a conflict, a whirlpool."[31] White was not persuaded to remain.

While in France with his family on his writing fellowship, White kept abreast of NAACP activities only sporadically. He did, however, call on Arthur Spingarn to review the manuscript he was writing on lynching, *Rope and Faggot: A Biography of Judge Lynch*. Arthur proved a frank critic of what he found to be the very disorganized work that White was about to send to his publisher. "The book I think falls between the idea of an objective treatise on lynching and the life of Judge Lynch and succeeds in being neither," he wrote in a lengthy letter that included many detailed suggestions for major changes of organization and approach. Advising him to greatly rewrite before sending to Alfred A. Knopf, Spingarn explained, "We are too good friends for me to substitute flattery for the honest and frank criticism you ask for."[32] The book was published in 1929 without wide acclaim, but it attracted respectable interest and included authoritative historical detail.

☖

As Joel pondered his wartime experiences and the postwar national mood, he became increasingly pessimistic about the future of the country. While a younger generation celebrated victory, a growing pacifism abroad, and cultural relaxation at home, Joel predicted a dim future. To his Amenia neighbor Lewis Mumford, 20 years his junior, he warned: "You liberals think that your liberal and pacifist world, with its peace treaties and disarmament conferences and material improvements, will last forever. I read history differently. You pacifists are preparing the way for bloodier wars. I predict that you will live to see the restoration of caste, and even slavery."[33] Later, as Nazi Germany advanced, Mumford would publicly proclaim: "His diagnosis was correct, and my youthful hopes were false."[34] Joel, however, had simply shrugged off any contrary general opinion, noting that "each man must find his own place of duty," and his was in camps and on battlefields. "For this, despite the reaction against war which is in all our hearts, I have no regrets."[35]

When he wrote about his cautionary views, as he did in an article in the *Freeman* titled "The Younger Generation: A New Manifesto," Joel's concerns netted little positive response. Yet he remained busy in a variety of literary projects, including a series of privately printed monographs he called "Troutbeck Leaflets," which showcased local history and literary thought, as well as a collection of poetry by his wife. Amy's poetic efforts increased, and her small book of verse, *Humility and Pride*, was published by Harcourt, Brace in 1926. Unfortunately, its reviews were far different from those that generally met Joel's work. The *Bookman* viewed it as demonstrating "amateurishness and prosiness of expression" and found in it "more pride than humility."[36]

In addition to a pace that fit the needs of his physical relapses, Spingarn enjoyed the country air, the Amenia community, and nearby friends. One of those, Pulitzer Prize–winning historian Van Wyck Brooks, described him as "proud, shy, cordial and winning. . . . His manner was quite natural, and he was really charming like some of his poems."[37] In 1924, when Brooks was struggling with his writing, Spingarn had gotten him a half-time editorial position at Harcourt, Brace. Although Brooks was fired after a year, they remained friends. Mumford, Brooks, Spingarn, and others enjoyed long conversations about art, literature, and the general state of the world—always with good-natured opinion and scholarly thought, but no rancorous debate. Joel renovated a group of cottages adjoining Troutbeck and invited various New York and Connecticut friends and literary scholars to spend summer vacations there. Mumford dubbed the community "a hamlet of ten houses." By the summer of 1928, Joel noted that Troutbeck was becoming a "literary centre," with Mumford, Brooks, and Edwin Arlington Robinson frequently writing there.[38]

Although Joel Spingarn's interaction with the NAACP occurred primarily at a distance during the 1920s, he was not without commitment. Importantly, some of that involvement, especially his financial acumen as the organization's treasurer, proved highly fruitful. As biographer Ross notes, he brought to that post an "enviable expertise in financial matters—especially the purchase and disposal of stocks and bonds." She writes, "his insistence on long-term investment of the NAACP's surplus funds was perhaps his greatest contribution." Spingarn also took the lead in establishing a five-member NAACP investment committee in 1926 and in working out ways to maximize the monies dedicated to legal defense and those accruing from life membership pledges.[39]

In their first decade of NAACP participation, the Spingarn brothers' financial contributions had occurred largely through Arthur's unpaid legal work and Joel and Amy's endowment of the Spingarn Medal. However, Joel and Amy began more frequent largesse in 1919 with a $500 contribution for an audit of the organization's books. They made additional contributions of $100 to $500 annually or more often throughout the 1920s. As part of a 1929

NAACP 20th-anniversary fund drive with a $200,000 goal, Joel and Amy donated $2,000 ($34,000 in 2022), which included $500 life memberships for Amy and Arthur.[40]

Especially eager to showcase contemporary Black achievements, Amy endowed the Amy Spingarn Prizes in support of "the contribution of the American Negro to American art and literature." The annual competition, administered by the *Crisis* among authors and artists whose work would be published in that journal, provided cash prizes for three winners in each category: fiction, verse, plays, essays, and illustrations. Early press coverage indicated the idea was hitting its mark. The *Emporia Gazette* in Kansas noted of the first-year competition: "Some notion of the progress that cultivated Negroes are making may be gathered from the recent award of the Amy Spingarn prizes for art and literature. Seven hundred Negro writers and artists competed."[41] This expansion of the *Crisis* somewhat mimicked the National Urban League's publication, *Opportunity: Journal of Negro Life*, founded and edited by Charles S. Johnson as an important outlet for Black expression in art and literature.

Regardless of his ability to contribute as both a financial donor and savvy advisor, Joel's limited action due to his recurring poor health left him frustrated. A letter from Amenia to Du Bois referred to Joel's "enforced subsidence into the side-lines among what you call the 'philanthropists.'" He concluded that "nothing the war did to me has caused me half as many regrets as my inability to go on in full vigor with the fight we once waged together."[42]

Later, however, perhaps making up for lost time from his postwar exhaustion and poor health, Joel's improved energy allowed him to embrace the last years of the decade more fully, enjoying family activities, entertainment, social events, and foreign travel. In 1926, he encouraged his daughters Hope (20 years old) and Honor (16 years old) to learn the French language and culture by enrolling them in a school in a beautiful château outside Paris. With a nearby lake and frequent student excursions to Paris theaters and shops, the daughters' summer experience at the Groslay School was followed by a European motor and train tour with their mother. Son Stephen, on summer break from Yale University, worked as a volunteer park ranger in Colorado at Mesa Verde National Park, while Edward finished his senior year at the Kent School in Connecticut.[43] Arthur's visits to Troutbeck allowed Joel, as NAACP treasurer, to keep abreast of various financial issues and consult from a distance. Arthur and his wife, Marion, soon leased and renovated a cottage Joel had named "Backwoods" on the Troutbeck property, which they used as a summer home.

With the means to travel well and often, Joel and Amy considered foreign countries not only interesting, but educational. By the spring of 1927, Joel's health allowed him to travel to London, where he visited friends and took in plays and museums. Son Stephen and daughter Hope took time off from their studies at Yale and Sweet Briar College, respectively, during the following fall and winter to take courses at the University of Grenoble in the French Alps. They were joined in Paris that spring by their mother, and their father sailed shortly after to meet them all in Spain. He and Amy were armed with conversational Spanish, which they had practiced prior to the trip, as well as Arthur Murray dance lessons.[44] Their youngest son, Edward, traveled to Europe the following summer before entering Bowdoin College.

Spingarn's improved health initially also allowed him to return to the Harcourt, Brace offices several afternoons a week during winter stays at his townhouse. There, he found himself enjoying "friendly social contacts and a convivial routine" as a "literary counsel."[45] Soon, however, as Great Depression realities challenged the ongoing efforts of the NAACP, Joel's return to precarious health limited his participation and increased his reliance on Arthur to represent his views at meetings. Unwilling to retreat from a life of duty and action to a life strictly of the mind, Joel still expected to return to full enjoyment of his varied interests at his country home and his useful involvement in the NAACP. He expressed as much in a 1931 lecture, later printed in the *Atlantic*, when he conceded that "the man of action never can become a poet or a philosopher." And he insisted that when that action-oriented man claims he will stop trying to do it all, "you know, of course, he is not going to."[46]

CHAPTER TEN

Ongoing Challenges and Final Change

Joel Spingarn had no intention of resuming an NAACP leadership role. When Moorfield Storey, the first and only NAACP president to date, died in 1929, Spingarn was approached by several association leaders about stepping in. He declined. A nominating committee deliberated and proposed additional names. The board of directors rejected the suggested candidates. During the next year, Spingarn did increase his active NAACP involvement by participating in the successful struggle against the confirmation of President Herbert Hoover's Supreme Court nominee, John J. Parker, a southern judge with a dismal record on racial equality. Finally, after more than a year without an NAACP president, Joel agreed to assume the office. However, he reminded the board of directors that "the association's Secretary is the executive officer of the NAACP."[1]

There were some objections to Spingarn's presidency, most prominently from racial activists who felt the time had come for African Americans to fill all the top NAACP posts. Among the Black press vocally preferring a Black NAACP president were the Harlem-based *Amsterdam News* and the *Chicago Bee*. Joel's status as Jewish and privileged also raised some doubts from outside the organization, as indicated in a letter to Du Bois from Robert L. Vann, the outspoken Black owner and editor of the *Pittsburgh Courier*:

> As to the presidency, it seems to me to be most unfortunate that a white man
> had to be elected. . . . I appreciate the financial help Mr. Spingarn has been to
> the association, but I can't appreciate his desire to be president as a reward for
> his financial help. Personally, I like the man; I like his attitude; but in dealing
> with cold facts, you must admit that the Christian world as we know it does
> not react too favorably to non-Christian leadership. Of course, Mr. Spingarn

> cannot help that he is a Jew, but his leadership will offer all the excuse certain white elements desire to justify their withdrawal of oral and financial support.

Du Bois quickly penned a brief reply: "The office of the President is a purely honorary position. His only duty is, if he so wishes, to preside at the annual mass meeting. . . . Both Mr. [James Weldon] Johnson and myself were heartily in favor of Mr. Spingarn's election."[2]

Johnson, after a year of leave on a Julius Rosenwald Fund writing fellowship, had resigned his post as NAACP executive secretary earlier in 1930. Walter White was elected to that position, and Roy Wilkins was hired as assistant secretary. Two years later, when Mary White Ovington moved from chair of the board of directors to the treasurer position, Joel Spingarn was additionally named board chair. Arthur continued in his roles as a vice president and chair of the legal committee. The association headquarters now accommodated full-time executives in departments from publicity to branches to office management, as well as assistants and secretaries.

With increased office staff and duties that were mostly ceremonial, Joel was able to renew his participation in a literary life. He served as a lecturer in literary criticism at the noted Middlebury College Bread Loaf School of English during the summer of 1931. There he joined visiting faculty from Harvard, Stanford, Dartmouth, Vanderbilt, and other universities in guiding an intensive graduate program. He also accepted the opportunity to prepare and deliver six lectures at the New School for Social Research in the same year. In those he addressed his own experiences as an activist and soldier and contemplated the need to reconcile those influences with the essential contributions of great poets and philosophers. Only one such lecture, "Politics and the Poet," has survived in print. In it, Joel describes a natural partnership among politics, poetry, philosophy, and religion—which he calls "the four noblest occupations of men." Politics represents the practical realm and the others the theoretical realm, but all four are important gifts. Politics, he insists, is "the gift to govern, an art quite as complete as the ability to write poetry or to think philosophy." He undoubtedly was considering his own interests in politics when he claimed that "the politician doesn't feel that sense that all is rotten in politics. He feels that the evil and good in the world are the very material with which he has to deal. He feels like the poet."[3]

The 1920s had been marked by significant legal victories, a sweeping antilynching campaign, and some successful lobbying in the US Congress. However, as the decade drew toward its close, the difficult financial realities of the Depression became a major focus. Paid memberships declined in the branches; the *Crisis*, with subscriptions dropping steadily, was no longer self-sustaining; and fundraising campaign pledges often did not materialize. Disagreements among NAACP leaders and staff about how to deal with budget tightening were inevitable, and Joel, the voice of financial reason during his years as treasurer, found himself at the forefront of heated discussions.

The control and form of the *Crisis*, long a subject of debate, prompted renewed argument during this financial stress. Joel agreed that change was necessary. In a lengthy letter from Amenia asking Arthur to represent his views at a meeting he could not attend, he reminded his brother that "Du Bois and *The Crisis* were the Association for the first ten years of its life," which gave the NAACP "the unique experience of having had for thirteen years an official organ, and an extremely valuable one, without a cent of expense." Nevertheless, he suggested a major overhaul, including a new editorial board that would "make the most drastic suggestions for reform, or rather complete alteration" in the publication's approach and purpose. Du Bois soon recognized that during the current struggle the NAACP would need to prop up the publication, "and if it did so, [the association] would have a right to a larger voice in its conduct and policy."[4]

The relationship between the two colleagues became difficult when Du Bois vocally insisted on a new NAACP economic program direction for Black citizens, which would take precedence over the organization's "mere appeal to justice and further effort at legal decision." He later claimed that Joel, his "nearest white friend," had tried to thwart the idea and was worried that "I was turning radical and dogmatic and even communistic." Spingarn agreed that current economic problems and the need for new approaches deserved NAACP attention, but he still insisted that the priority was "racial equality for the Negro . . . equal and unrestricted admission to the duties and discipline of American life." He may have reflected his own Jewish and privileged roots when he supported the idea of a broader and proactive NAACP program, but insisted that the organization continue to recognize that "the chief danger is caste, a quite different thing, and a far more insidious enemy and a far more unshakable master than money, which to a certain extent is within the reach of all men."[5]

Joel also fretted about Walter White's financial management. The life membership drive started by Spingarn in 1927 had yielded few fully paid memberships by 1930, although some were paying on installments. While Joel had intended the funds to be in a long-term account, White and others argued they should be placed in the general fund for current expenses. In early 1930, working with auditors and the board of directors, Arthur Spingarn managed to get a separate account established for each designated "special fund." However, as the general fund declined, White began charging salaries to the various separate accounts.[6]

Although friendly with White and sometimes a mentor in his fiction and nonfiction literary efforts, Joel was convinced that the secretary was simply not able or not willing to lead efforts to stretch the shrinking association resources. In a 1932 letter to Arthur about his views on waste, Joel asked his brother to approach White about reducing expenses by adjusting the 72-page annual report:

> This is too extravagant for these times. I suggest that we cut the size in half, use cheaper paper, use no blank pages, use as inexpensive printing as is consistent with neatness. The report ought to look a little impoverished. Will you take this up with Walter immediately? I am afraid he does not know how to economize. There are leaders for deflationist times, and I wonder if he will ever be able to adapt his psyche to the new state of the world.[7]

Regardless of various differences in priorities, Joel's return to NAACP activities put him in the role of go-to confidant for several longtime associates. Ovington, Du Bois, Arthur Spingarn, and others counted on Joel's reason and influence. Walter White sent him a note marked "personal" to share his discomfort at treatment he had received from some board members. Du Bois appealed to Spingarn for personal loans. When Ovington convinced him to support her as treasurer and to add serving as board chair to his own tasks, she explained: "We think alike about a good many things; you have helped me more than anyone I know to preserve such idealism as I have."[8]

⚖

Both Spingarn brothers continued active and enjoyable lives beyond their NAACP leadership. Arthur traveled frequently concerning his book- and print-collecting interests. Joel enjoyed not only family life and a country estate, but also literary work and an impressive Upper East Side townhouse, which Roy Wilkins described as "a small palace."[9] Joel and Amy also found time for generosity to individuals in need. At least one such contribution would have memorable implications well into the future. James Weldon Johnson, teaching at Fisk University after resigning his NAACP position, asked the couple to consider a donation to a very promising, but nearly penniless student so that she could continue beyond her freshman year.[10] Their gift to Fanny McConnell prevented her from dropping out of college by fully funding her sophomore year. She later transferred to and graduated from the University of Iowa after receiving a full scholarship. A talented and dedicated activist, after graduation she founded the Negro People's Theatre in Chicago and wrote for the *Chicago Defender*. When she moved to New York, she became assistant to the director of the National Urban League and married a hopeful writer, Ralph Ellison. She edited and typed his handwritten manuscript, which was published as *Invisible Man* to international acclaim in 1952 and won the National Book Award the next year. Fanny McConnell Ellison died in 2005 at age 93.

Arthur's bibliophilic interests led him to review books by Black authors in a regular column for the *Crisis*. He was doggedly determined to cover all of them—an undertaking that grew from reviewing about 40 to more than 100 books a year during his 30 years at the task. The effort multiplied as he received enormous quantities of correspondence from hopeful essayists, novelists, poets, and songwriters, who longed for their work to be reviewed or for their ideas to inspire encouragement. Arthur continued his book collecting through his nearly annual trips to England, where he was a member of the London Bibliographical Society and an incorporator of the Oxford Bibliographical Society. His wife, Marion, continued her social work in New York after wartime duties in Washington, DC. She worked in protective services for low-income young women in dangerous circumstances and served very much on the front line. "She worked 18 hours a day," Arthur later recalled. "In the middle of the night she'd hear of some young girl who was being kept in some place, and she'd dress and go there. . . . She carried a police whistle, but she always left her gun at home."[11]

⚖

Once a high-spirited activist for the early NAACP purposes of racial equality and legal justice, Joel Spingarn became somewhat discouraged, even bored, with what he viewed as merely the continuation of earlier organizational emphases. Surviving the war and Depression and tending to the needs of various colleagues were not enough. He explained in a letter to Ovington:

> If I were a lawyer like my brother, I should find some difficult and interesting question involved in every one of our successive "cases," and I should hardly miss the cement of a programme. But as it is, I am not interested in a succession of cases. . . . Now we have only cases, no programme, and no hope. Every

effort I have made to try to put this hope into our work by framing a pro-
gramme has been ignored or thwarted by the Secretary or by the Board.[12]

The programs he had in mind included addressing social and political access issues among Black citizens through equality in education, fair employment practices, and nondiscrimination in trades and professions—"fuller
opportunity, wider opportunity."[13] He warned against an overemphasis on
the vital economic problems of the time, however. In his address to the 1932
NAACP annual conference, he insisted that the major issue for the association must be the much more encompassing "battle for racial equality."[14] In
this he represented a centrist position—not as far left as Du Bois and some
others pushing a wide-ranging economic support agenda, but not as far right
as those who felt that if equal rights happened, economic issues would resolve
themselves. He was not alone among NAACP leaders seeking new emphases,
but he was not in the majority. Sensing that the association was unlikely to
embrace his preferred agenda, he sent his formal resignation as president
and board chair to secretary White and the board in March 1933. However,
several months of machinations and pleas by White, former secretary Johnson, and various board members convinced him to remain in the presidency
and to serve as board chair until a new chair could be appointed.

Current frustrations and questions about the future paved the way for a
second Amenia conference at Spingarn's Troutbeck estate. It was held for
three days in August 1933 to discuss possible next steps related to racial problems and people of color in the United States and beyond. Invitations were
sent to well-educated Black thinkers and writers, early career lawyers, university leaders, social and political activists, and others. Thirty-three attended,
with a median age of 30. Among them were familiar and highly regarded
individuals, including Ralph Bunche, E. Franklin Frazier, Charles Hamilton
Houston, and Louis Redding. Joel Spingarn, Walter White, Roy Wilkins, and
W. E. B. Du Bois represented the NAACP.

While economic issues and their effect on the Black population were
widely discussed at the conference, and the idea that Black labor should be
more closely tied to the very activist labor movement met agreement in principle, no clear action path emerged. Louis Redding, the first Black lawyer to
be admitted to the Delaware bar, was satisfied with much of the meeting.
However, he noted to Joel that many participants were hampered by the assimilationist tendencies of a Black class "infused with middle-class American 'success philosophy' . . . so securely wedged in a comfortable economic

Amenia conference, 1933. Photograph by Carl Van Vechten, Yale Collection of American Literature, Beinecke Rare Book and Manuscript Library; used with permission of the Van Vechten Trust

status that it is difficult for them to remember that there is a great mass of Negroes who are poor, ignorant, uncounseled and exploited."[15] Biographer Joyce Ross concludes that Joel "was greatly disappointed because the conferees had failed to provide a concrete plan for implementing their conclusions." Yet James Weldon Johnson, writing from Fisk University to thank Amy Spingarn for conference photos she had sent, observed that "the 2nd Amenia Conference, like the 1st, goes down as an important event in American Negro history."[16]

A general clamor for change from inside and outside the NAACP prompted the board to appoint the Committee on Future Plan and Program, which would ultimately pave the way for the inclusion of at least some new directions. Those directions would be shaped by the ideas of what historian Beth Tompkins Bates labels "a new crowd" of younger and more militant Black people:

"The moderate approach of the old guard relied on making appeals or seeking legal redress for individuals; the new crowd on collective demands."[17]

Du Bois, pessimistic about anything short of profound change, found the inconclusive Amenia conference results disappointing but not unexpected, noting "the turmoil and contradiction of our discussion. Our argument was indeterminate and our resolutions contradictory."[18] His preference for proactive social and economic outreach programs supportive of working-class Black people had led him to favor a clear distinction between segregation and discrimination—voluntarily pulling together for improved opportunity versus exclusion based on skin color. In the *Crisis* of January 1934, he insisted that voluntary segregation, often viewed as promoting Black nationalism, could boost individual success by enabling "colored people to work with each other, to co-operate with each other, to live with each other." His editorial encouraged Black laborers and farmers to separate from integrated work collaboratives and form their own group economies.[19] Walter White had wide support in objecting to Du Bois's stance on segregation, including that of Joel Spingarn, who told Du Bois that in touting segregation in the *Crisis* he had "hit below the belt."[20]

In guiding a formal board response to the segregation question, Joel again was in the role of calming, if not clearly accommodating, differing interests. He insisted that the NAACP's response avoid a "no segregation" tone. Instead, noting the success of many Black churches, colleges, and clubs, he suggested two elements: "a general conviction that segregation is an evil" and yet "complete liberty of action in regard to specific cases."[21] Shortly after, the board voted for a resolution stating its opposition to "enforced" color or race segregation. However, it did not address Joel and Arthur's suggestion that some Black institutions and endeavors could be acknowledged as practical deviations from zero segregation tolerance. Arthur denounced the resolution as "silly," while Joel labeled it "weak."[22]

Already lecturing as a visiting faculty member at Atlanta University and experiencing new limitations on his editorial independence in the *Crisis* from a distance, Du Bois had threatened to resign from his NAACP post several months earlier. As he became publicly critical of NAACP policies in the *Crisis,* the board sought ways to curb his editorial control. In a letter to Arthur Spingarn, who served on the *Crisis* committee, Du Bois fumed that if White and Wilkins had the ultimate power over editorial affairs, "I resign. Moreover, I will not have a *Crisis* board of which Roy Wilkins is a member. He has neither the brains nor guts to be a member of any board." However, Du Bois noted to Arthur: "I do wish you would stay on the board as you are almost the only level-head that we have." Although Joel and Arthur met with Du Bois in Atlanta and New York to attempt some compromise, if not actually change his mind, Du Bois resigned his NAACP *Crisis* editorship and board membership in June 1934.[23] He took a position as chair of the Department of Sociology at Atlanta University. Roy Wilkins became the acting editor of the *Crisis*.

Just four months after the Du Bois resignation, the Committee on Future Plan and Program submitted its preliminary report. Both Spingarn brothers and Ovington were committee members, but sensing they were far outnumbered by younger activist members, they had not attended recent meetings. When the report was issued, Joel took on the challenge of diplomacy between the forces supporting an extreme swing to the left in economic and social programming and those seeking only limited change. The report was aimed at creating a comprehensive labor and political action program for Black and white workers, including the establishment of workers' and farmers' councils for united action in areas such as "participation in strikes lockouts, and labor demonstrations." As Joel scribbled changes onto his copy of the report, he was determined to maintain the centrality of the organization's historic purposes of equal rights and nondiscrimination while also reaching out to include some consideration of economic needs.[24] He clarified at the 1935 NAACP annual conference that while he favored no extreme change in NAACP efforts, he did view the organization as "young enough, flexible enough to conserve what is best of its old heritage and to try new methods and new ideals.... Now even if the economic problem becomes an important problem of our organization, there will still be a need for the old role of the NAACP."[25]

The preliminary report of the Committee on Future Plan and Program also tackled issues of organizational structure and administration, calling for decentralization of the national office and a greater voice for the branches and rank-and-file members. By the time the board of directors, still chaired by Joel Spingarn, revised and adopted the report, there was some voice and vote beyond the national office and at least a nod to a slow path of unity with organized labor. It was a compromise among factions and an acknowledgment of the need to expand on the NAACP's original purposes. Perhaps exhausted by various efforts of the Depression years, Joel announced the end of his board chairmanship by 1935. However, he maintained his titular role as president and continued his activities on the association's budget committee and the committee on administration.

⚖

Arthur Spingarn's role as chair of the legal committee had evolved into a steady stream of advice to Walter White and Roy Wilkins about handling legal questions brought to their attention from the branches and elsewhere. Arthur's advice largely concerned which legal cases to take on, which to leave to the branches, what approaches might or might not work, which lawyers should be involved, and what financial implications were on the horizon. From his private law practice at 19 West 44th Street and at NAACP headquarters on Fifth Avenue, Spingarn acted as somewhat of a gatekeeper. He reviewed possible legal matters and advised that branches take up suggested cases, that cases did not look promising for the complainants, that only advice was warranted, or that more information or documentation was necessary. Legal efforts had evolved; they were as much a matter of response as of planned strategy, which Walter White observed was the result of "limited resources and the constant succession of cases which the Association had to handle on an emergency basis." Noting Spingarn's generous volunteer work as the legal committee chair, White added, "it was kind of a joke between us that he handled his own private law practice during such periods as he was not engaged in working without compensation for the NAACP."[26]

Arthur's own practice inevitably included friends and colleagues who knew him, or of him, through some aspect of his NAACP work. White was particularly active in asking him to confer with friends about financial issues and potential contracts. Additionally, Spingarn frequently advised Du Bois on numerous personal activities. He later maintained, "I was his personal lawyer . . . of course without remuneration. And, believe me, he had plenty of trouble, chiefly with the ladies. He was a great ladies' man."[27] Other, less frequent clients with ties to Spingarn's NAACP work included William Sinclair, Langston Hughes, and Emmett Scott. He also took on tax work for Joel's friends Van Wyck Brooks and Lewis Mumford. Undoubtedly, one of his most interesting incidents of legal wrangling was a question of authorship, ownership, and copyright between Langston Hughes and Zora Neale Hurston. The two Harlem Renaissance literary notables were good friends who started collaborating on a play in 1930. They only had a somewhat solid first act of *Mule Bone*, a comedy about Black life, when Hughes received some encouraging feedback from a theatrical producer near Philadelphia. He contacted Hurston about any further progress, and she informed him that she had revised, ignored his suggestions, and made the play her own. Later, she claimed that Hughes immediately threatened her that "his friend Mr. Spingarn was a lawyer and a good one."[28]

In October 1930, Zora Neale Hurston copyrighted the play as sole author and continued to work on it and remove early contributions by Langston Hughes. Inevitably, accusations and tempers flared between the two authors, and Hughes soon consulted Arthur Spingarn. Although Spingarn undoubtedly did not want to be in the middle of emotionally charged disagreements, he landed there anyway. He made Hurston a compromise offer of two-thirds of the royalties and passed along to his client her insistence that she be sole author. Spingarn was soon visited by famed writer and philosopher Alain Locke in vigorous support of Hurston as the play's author. After additional letters and meetings on the subject led to only more claims and complaints on both sides, Spingarn must have been greatly relieved when the script and the idea of interesting producers in it were abandoned. In a final letter, Hurston warned him of "certain things I have in my possession" and concluded: "I think it would be lovely for your client to be a play-wright but I'm afraid that I am too tight to make him one at my expense." The relationship between the authors was severed, and the play was not performed until 1991.[29]

As NAACP leaders and members reexamined the organization's goals and functions during trying financial times, the legal committee's structure and work also came under some scrutiny. Although the committee had long been a small group of close-knit volunteer advisors examining potential cases and how to handle them, Walter White pushed committee chair Arthur Spingarn to increase its numbers and diversity during the 1930s. Felix Frankfurter and Clarence Darrow were added, as were two distinguished lawyers involved with the American Civil Liberties Union, Arthur Garfield Hays and Morris Ernst. But the committee's sole Black lawyer, James Cobb of Washington, DC, had resigned in 1926. This presented a dilemma for Spingarn. He well understood the desire for diversification and often promoted it at the level of NAACP branch legal work. However, he maintained that the larger, precedent-setting cases required lawyers of national standing and well-seasoned expertise. The great majority of those were white. When White, the NAACP acting secretary in 1931, proposed two Black lawyers to be added to the legal committee, Spingarn did agree to one of them: T. Gillis Nutter, a state legislator instrumental in desegregation actions in West Virginia. Later, however, when White suggested two additional Black attorneys, Spingarn countered with suggestions for adding white lawyers to the committee. Spingarn was, according to legal historians Meier and Rudwick, "still skeptical of adding young men who as yet lacked a national reputation."[30]

Nevertheless, even the considered and careful legal committee chair soon recognized that a growing number of young Black attorneys were making their marks at Ivy League law schools and in their subsequent legal careers. Four of those were appointed to the NAACP legal committee in the summer of 1932: a Harvard Law School graduate and the visionary dean of Howard Law School, Charles Hamilton Houston; Ohio attorney Jesse S. Heslip, then president of the Black National Bar Association; Harvard Law School graduate and prominent Delaware civil rights advocate Louis Redding; and N. J. Frederick, who was older than the others and the only civil rights lawyer practicing in Columbia, South Carolina. With the addition the following year of two more Black members, William Hastie and Homer Brown, the legal committee finally reached nearly equal numbers of white and Black attorneys.[31] Walter White later recalled that the new composition of the committee, with its added youth and diversity, enabled the association to begin "a broad frontal attack on the basic causes of discrimination instead of waiting to handle the manifestations."[32]

In 1935 the NAACP created the role of special counsel, its first salaried legal employee. White prevailed upon Arthur Spingarn to nominate Charles H. Houston to the position. A brilliant lawyer whose success while on the legal committee had included several stunning court cases, Houston was initially engaged on a part-time basis. His commitment to Black leadership in struggles for Black justice and equality, especially aimed at the reality of caste in southern states, would shape much of the NAACP work in the coming years.

Although Arthur Spingarn remained chair of what was now called the Legal Department, his court case decision-making involvement took a back seat to Houston, White, and some of the new Legal Department members. Determined to initiate a proactive legal agenda, Houston added lawyers with branch-level success. His efforts quickly yielded, according to historian Patricia Sullivan, "an active network of lawyers working at the grass roots, prepared to advise, support, and implement the legal campaign."[33] Recognizing, or perhaps trumpeting, the passing of the legal baton, the association hosted a testimonial dinner in 1935 to honor Spingarn's many years as chair of the legal committee. Houston served as toastmaster for the occasion, and supporters of equal rights who attended included NAACP friends and staff from throughout the years.[34]

If there was any doubt that the new guard lawyers could make an immediate and positive impact, that was quickly erased by a stunning victory in opening the University of Maryland Law School to Black students. Donald Gaines Murray's application had been rejected at the law school in early 1935 due to his race, just as Thurgood Marshall's had been earlier at the same law school. Marshall had then become a brilliant student of Charles Houston at Howard Law School and upon graduation returned to Baltimore to practice law. When Houston heard about Murray's rejection, he called on the 27-year-old Marshall to assist in the legal battle to desegregate the Maryland school. They won their case for Murray's admission in Baltimore City Court. Next, they won in the Maryland Court of Appeals, making history as the first such ruling. Alain Locke proclaimed the outcome "a tide turning victory."[35] Murray graduated from the University of Maryland Law School in 1938 and built a successful career practicing law in Baltimore.

Several years later, Houston developed a case against the University of Missouri Law School when it refused admission to Lincoln University graduate Lloyd Gaines on racial grounds but offered him funding to attend an out-of-state integrated law school. The case was argued by Houston at the Supreme Court in 1938, while Woodrow Wilson appointee Justice James McReynolds swiveled his chair to turn his back on the Black lawyer. After the 6–2 victory for equal educational opportunity, Missouri and other states were required to admit students to the same or equal in-state educational training, ending the practice of funding Black students to undertake programs in other states.[36] Ironically, Lloyd Gaines never took advantage of the win. In a mystery that remains unsolved, he moved to Chicago several months after the Supreme Court ruling and disappeared without a trace. However, the case undoubtedly energized the NAACP and others involved in the struggle to remove racial bias from educational opportunity at all levels.

In late 1938, Houston moved back to Washington, DC. Thurgood Marshall was appointed co–special counsel in charge of the New York Legal Department of the NAACP.

⚖️

Although Arthur's work with NAACP legal activities became less demanding and Joel's board chair duties began to wind down, the brothers nevertheless continued to busily address multiple ongoing issues of racial equality. Two areas in particular found them frequently involved in lobbying state government representatives, US congressional delegations, cabinet members, and President Franklin D. Roosevelt. One was the ongoing fight for a federal antilynching bill. The other was the determination to secure the equal inclusion of Black people in various New Deal efforts aimed at relief and recovery for American workers. The Spingarns' familiarity with Roosevelt, who took office in 1933, certainly didn't hurt. Joel, who had cooled on partisan political activities for some time, had gotten to know the Hyde Park Roosevelts as neighbors living about 25 miles west of his estate in Amenia. Arthur later recalled, "FDR was an old friend of our family. We knew FDR before he ran for state senator, before he amounted to anything."[37] While working for the NAACP, suffrage, public hygiene, and other causes, Joel and Arthur had numerous opportunities to interact with Roosevelt while he served in the New York State Senate and then as governor of New York.

Roosevelt's early New Deal program efforts could easily work to the detriment or exclusion of Black interests if not crafted to ensure equal treatment, fair wages, admission to training programs, and union membership access. Throughout his first administration and beyond, Roosevelt heard from the NAACP, most directly from Joel, on race-related issues in programs of the Agricultural Adjustment Administration, the Federal Housing Administration, the Public Works Administration, the Civilian Conservation Corps, and others. Fortunately, the case for an equal share of New Deal benefits for Black people was supported by top Roosevelt appointees, such as Secretary of Interior Harold Ickes, a former NAACP Chicago branch president; Secretary of Labor Frances Perkins; and Secretary of Commerce Harry Hopkins. Undoubtedly, Eleanor Roosevelt's open and uncompromising support for Black Americans, expressed in many conversations with NAACP leaders, was also greatly influential.[38] Arthur Spingarn noted that those individuals, especially Eleanor, were more effective on racial issues than the politically cautious president. He maintained: "F.D.R. was interested, but he wouldn't sacrifice himself." He described a visit he made with Joel about ensuring equal Black consideration in some New Deal initiatives. But Roosevelt demurred: "Arthur, now I'll tell you, I'd be glad to do this, but it wouldn't help you." Arthur later concluded that Roosevelt "wasn't willing to sacrifice his popularity in any way. Of course, she [Eleanor] was, and of course she was hated in the South."[39]

President Roosevelt proved to be similarly politically motivated in response to ongoing lobbying by the Spingarn brothers and other NAACP leaders for federal antilynching legislation. A bill first drafted by the legal committee had won the sponsorship of Colorado senator Edward Costigan and New York senator Robert Wagner. Two days of Senate hearings on the bill in 1934 centered on the horrors of lynching and the inaction of local officials. Arthur Spingarn testified that more than 3,500 lynchings had occurred since 1900. Only 67 offenders had been indicted, and a mere 12 had been convicted.[40] Although Roosevelt had publicly condemned lynching, he would not take on the southern strength in Congress by favoring the Costigan-Wagner bill. He did grant Joel Spingarn a personal interview on lynching concerns in 1937, but the issue was quickly set aside for other topics raised by the president.[41] When the president was visited by Walter White and an all-Black delegation the following year, Roosevelt applauded their efforts toward an antilynching law but insisted that any public support from him would only hinder their cause. He maintained that lynching was something up to the states to confront and curtail. Without the president's backing and with vigorous southern bloc filibustering, federal antilynching bills continued to fail to pass.[42]

⚖

While Joel retained his title of president and his membership on the board of directors, his active participation in NAACP matters slowed greatly in the second half of the 1930s. He and Amy were immersed in community activities and interests in Amenia, as well as in following the varied activities of their four children in young adulthood. Edward was pursuing a PhD in economics at Harvard. Hope, who had studied at Sweet Briar College and the Sorbonne, was testing her acting skills with a few small roles in Broadway plays. Stephen, a 1934 graduate of the University of Arizona Law School, had begun his career as a legislative lawyer at the US Treasury Department. Honor, an artist and textile designer, took part in various New Deal activities in New York, such as painting frescoes for WPA projects. She was married at Troutbeck in 1937 to Carl Tranum. While the Spingarn estate continued as a welcoming arena for weekend visitors from New York and Connecticut, as well as Amenia neighbors, Joel's growing passion for gardening also consumed much of his time in the country.

Always a deep diver into subjects that demanded lengthy study and experiment, Joel became intensely fascinated by clematis, a flowering vine of at least 300 species and scores of hybrids. Eventually leading to his recognition as a national and international expert, this particular pursuit stemmed from his realization that the plant had been "neglected" to the point where "not a single arboretum, botanic garden, or agricultural college in the United States has a representative collection of clematis plants growing on its grounds."[43] This was an oversight he began to tackle on his own estate. His additional reading on the subject and his attendance at meetings of the Horticultural

Society of New York and numerous other gardening groups kept him abreast of the long history and current activities concerning clematis in Europe, Asia, and the United States.

As his understanding and his garden grew, Joel also produced a steady stream of writing on the subject. Between 1933 and 1938, he authored more than a dozen articles in publications including *National Horticultural Magazine, Landscape Architecture Magazine, House and Garden, Horticulture, Gardeners' Chronicle, Garden Digest,* and *Flower Grower.* He widely distributed a pamphlet titled *Clematis at Troutbeck: Tentative Check List of Species, Varieties, and Hybrids.* It listed nearly 100 named types on his estate and an additional 45 "large flowering hybrids." Horticulturalists from near and far visited his gardens, and he received numerous accolades and awards from gardening clubs and societies, including a gold medal at the 1937 International Flower Show. One reader of his work in *Gardener's Journal* later wrote that "his botanical descriptions practically hypnotize me." Lewis Mumford later described these years of his friend's growing frustration with social and political thought and increasing involvement with horticulture. Mumford fumed that "toward the end of his life, this soldier and thinker was known throughout the world as the chief authority on—clematis!"[44]

Joel had voted for Franklin Roosevelt in 1932, but his involvement expanded to actively campaigning for the president's 1936 reelection. Although not in an official NAACP capacity, he spoke for Roosevelt to many largely Black audiences in several states.[45] He took pride in the upward swing toward Democrats among Black voters in 1936. Throughout 1937 and early 1938, he also included in his NAACP presidential duties attendance at a number of committee meetings, especially in the areas of budget and administration. He had planned to spend time as a visiting lecturer at Atlanta University during the fall of 1938, but a major and final illness—diagnosed as a brain tumor—left any such activity impossible.

At 64 years old, Joel Spingarn died on July 26, 1939. He was interred in a plot he had purchased a year earlier at Poughkeepsie Rural Cemetery in his beloved Dutchess County.[46] His will included a $20,000 trust to perpetuate the annual Spingarn Medal. NAACP colleagues elected Amy Spingarn to fulfill the remainder of his term on the board of directors, and Arthur succeeded his brother as president of the association.

W. E. B. Du Bois soon dedicated his autobiography to "Joel Spingarn, Scholar and Knight." In it, he summarized their relationship succinctly and frankly: "I do not think that any other white man ever touched me emotionally so closely as Joel Spingarn. He was one of those vivid, enthusiastic, but clear-thinking idealists which from age to age the Jewish race has given the world. . . . I was both fascinated by his character and antagonized by some of his quick and positive judgments."[47]

CHAPTER ELEVEN

A New Era for Old Soldiers

When Arthur Spingarn assumed the presidency of the NAACP in 1940, that position was still much more of an honorary role than a leadership calling. Nevertheless, he pledged that during his tenure the organization would not swerve in the slightest "from its courageous, militant and intelligent work to obtain for the Negroes of the country their full manhood rights awarded to all Americans by the Constitution of the United States."[1] He retained his title as chair of the NAACP Legal Department, and that soon changed to "president."

The 30 members of the 1940 legal committee hailed from 18 NAACP branches. They included Joel's son Stephen Spingarn, a recent law school graduate. The NAACP special counsel, 32-year-old Thurgood Marshall, guided their activities. Early in 1940, Arthur Spingarn, Marshall, and others launched plans for reorganizing their legal efforts under the independent NAACP Legal Defense and Educational Fund, Inc. (LDEF). Spingarn succinctly stated that "its purpose was to get tax exempt funds."[2] The NAACP had undoubtedly lost substantial contributions due to its lobbying and propaganda activities, which disqualified it for tax-deductible donations.

Marshall drafted the LDEF corporate charter, and Spingarn set about lobbying among New York Bar Association members and others for its passage into corporate status by the New York Department of State. Spingarn and six other NAACP board members, three Black and three white, constituted the original LDEF self-perpetuating board of directors. Spingarn served as its president for 17 years, while also serving as NAACP president. Legal scholar and later LDEF director Jack Greenberg writes that although "ultimate power" remained with the LDEF directors, "they soon turned over matters almost entirely to Thurgood Marshall, their chief counsel, who was closely attuned to the needs and aspirations of black America." He also notes that "Marshall was personal friends with most members of the board. Arthur Spingarn spoke of Thurgood as a son."[3]

Spingarn's concern about racial inequality impacting US relations with other countries moved him well beyond his frequent foreign travel for artistic and literary collecting. Since earlier visits related to the occupation of Haiti, he had remained keenly aware that prejudice and discrimination did not stop at national boundaries. After a 1941 trip to the Panama Canal Zone, a decades-long US territory, he was determined to convince President Franklin Roosevelt to act against long-standing racial discrimination there. He spoke of it on a visit to the White House and wrote to Roosevelt that segregation in the Canal Zone was "substantially the same as that existing in the lower South." Black workers from the United States, the West Indies, and elsewhere were limited to "separate commissaries, living quarters, railroad accommodations and even lavatories established by the Canal authorities. . . . a colored man is subject to arrest if he enters a white commissary." Spingarn also noted salary and wage discrimination and called on the president to mount an investigation and plan for corrective measures.[4] Although Spingarn had a long and friendly relationship with Roosevelt, there is no indication that he was able to achieve any influence in the matter of the Canal Zone.

As US involvement in World War II loomed, the NAACP began to consider the consequences for Black troops, officers, and trainees. Membership and branches experienced a huge growth spurt upon the 1941 US entry into the war, highlighting a time of questioning how military forces and civilian support efforts would confront issues of racial equality. Historian Patricia Sullivan views the impressive NAACP expansion as a response to "the massive mobilization of troops in the segregated armed forces, the frustration experienced by blacks in their efforts to obtain defense jobs, and the tightening constraints of segregation in urban areas buckling under the weight of migration."[5]

Racialized approaches to military preparedness were allowed to follow local customs with only limited federal government intervention. The US Marine Corps remained strictly white until mid-1942, and while Black men were present in army and navy training camps, segregation generally found them assigned to the most crowded barracks and barred from certain facilities. Black pilot training was confined to Tuskegee Air Base, and the American Red Cross segregated its blood banks. Soldiers training at bases in the

South were regularly subjected to humiliation and refusals of service when they ventured into nearby communities. Mary White Ovington, still the NAACP treasurer and an active board member, noted that "negro soldiers were segregated in buses, at motion pictures, in shops, and at counters in drugstores."[6]

William Hastie, a Roosevelt judicial appointee in 1937 and then dean of the Howard University School of Law, served as a civilian advisor to US Secretary of War Henry Stimson from 1940 to early 1943. He resigned in protest when he could get only very limited action from government officials regarding Black trainees' treatment and assignments. He was awarded the Spingarn Medal by the NAACP that year. The idea of racial equality had received a boost from President Roosevelt's Executive Order 8802 (1941), which created the Fair Employment Practices Committee and prohibited discrimination in hiring by government agencies and contractors. However, according to Ovington, that move and other hopeful signs "presaged no general changes in the War Department's attitude. The Army did not intend to break with the past."[7]

After US entry into the war, Black soldiers brought more and more complaints of discrimination and abuse to the attention of the NAACP. Sullivan found "there was an overwhelming large number of cases involving court-martial and dishonorable discharge, often for protesting or resisting discriminatory treatment."[8] Racism ranged from assigning Black soldiers the most menial work to falsely accusing them of crimes and misdemeanors. Not surprisingly, questions surfaced among Black citizens about fighting for a country where they were held in far lower regard than their fellow white citizens. Spingarn penned an essay addressed to doubting Black men about doing their part in wartime even amid racial discrimination. In "If I Were a Negro," he was both candidly empathetic and insistently patriotic:

> If I were a Negro, I would sincerely believe that my attitude toward the War would not be materially changed. I probably would be a little more bitter about the hollow hypocrisies of the loudmouthed fascists among us who prate about democracy without believing in or practicing it, but I would feel that with all its faults and despite the discriminations, cruelties and injustices from which I suffer under our democracy, that democracy as practiced in America is infinitely better than any system that would prevail if the Axis won. . . . That democracy which America proclaims and so often fails to live up to will some day be not merely the hope of the world but a reality.
>
> I would know that under Hitler or Hirohito I could not even continue to

strive for this ideal; I could not even voice my protests through a *Negro Digest*. So, if I were a Negro I would still believe that there is no other possible course open to me than an all out participation in the War . . . for I would know that victory cannot be won without it.[9]

When he sent this piece to *Negro Digest* for that publication's "If I Were a Negro" column by white guest authors, he quickly heard from the editor that it would appear in an upcoming issue, although no evidence has been found that it was actually published.[10]

Also during the war, Spingarn drafted an essay to Jewish citizens about their failure to truly push for an end to racial inequality for Black people. Titled "The Jew as a Racial Minority," it was his first forceful effort to address complicated discrimination issues related to both Black and Jewish citizens, and he concluded that "so far, the Jewish contribution toward justice for the Negro has been unorganized, ineffective and inadequate." Although he noted some outstanding exceptions among prominent Jewish philanthropists, he also said that rising antisemitism, so vividly on display in Germany and elsewhere, should be heightening Jewish activism regarding racial inequality. However, he found that Jews "rarely seem to have realized that there have been no slurs made against Negroes that have not had their counterparts in antisemitic propaganda. . . . The same forces that have excluded Jews from certain employments are the blood brothers of those that bar the doors to Negroes." Discouraged by his observations, he minced no words:

> My own experience in the South has shown me far too often that the Jew has accepted fully the southern white attitude of Negro inferiority with its accompanying exploitation. . . . Pathetically, the Negroes have been equally naïve, and antisemitic feeling is widespread and growing among them. There appears to be little likelihood of a real contribution until all Jewish leaders unite in recognizing that race prejudice is the common problem of all minority groups and further realize that, given a chance, the Negro, as well as the Jew, has every potentiality of all mankind. They must believe and teach that the Negro in the United States and in the New World we are fighting for is rightfully entitled to full political, economic, educational and social equality. . . . Only when the Jew becomes the voice and symbol of race justice can he expect justice anywhere in the world; only when he grants freedom can he hope for freedom.[11]

The largely honorary nature of his two NAACP positions, along with increasing numbers of full-time leaders and lawyers in the organization, left

Spingarn with a great deal more time for other pursuits. Most consuming was his lifelong interest in literature. He continued his annual review of books by Black authors for the *Crisis*, which appeared from 1936 to 1968. And he maintained his efforts to collect rare books, prints, essays, poems, and musical compositions. His regular trips to London—sometimes three in one year—allowed him to comb through bookstores and libraries and to continue his contacts in bibliographic societies.

Long known for showcasing the literary and artistic accomplishments of centuries of American Black people, Spingarn also was determined to extend recognition to other countries and continents. In his 1940 commencement speech at Talladega College, he noted that the great achievements of Black US citizens "do not by any means represent the whole or even greater part of Negro achievement in the western world. In Europe and Latin America, for centuries Negroes have been writing continually and ably in practically every language and on every conceivable subject." His many examples came from his own collection of rare, often singular, literary triumphs, ranging from the verses of African-born American poet Phillis Wheatley to the novels of the Brazilian Machado de Assis.[12] The large and growing library at Spingarn's home in Gramercy Park housed at least 5,000 works on floor-to-ceiling shelves. They included single sheets, books, pamphlets, musical compositions, and multivolume works by Black men and women in Arabic, Latin, Spanish, French, German, Dutch, Portuguese, Russian, English, and Creole. The oldest was a volume of poetry by Juan Latino, an enslaved man in Granada, which was published in 1573.[13] Determined to acknowledge literature as a long-standing achievement among Black people, he had earlier reminded readers that "Negro authors have written in almost every language, in almost every country, on almost every conceivable subject, and for more than a thousand years."[14]

In his search for all the literature relevant to his collection, the dogged bibliophile visited private and public libraries, churches, shops, and attics at home and abroad. He frequently corresponded with authors, editors, scholars, and collectors in Africa, the West Indies, South and Central America, and the United States. He also welcomed visiting scholars to his home library to consult resources they could not find elsewhere. While he especially treasured rare early works, Spingarn's library also included more recent writings by Frederick Douglass, P. B. S. Pinchback, Benjamin Brawley, and others. He was particularly proud to note that his friend Langston Hughes was the first Black person in a century "to earn his living solely through his literary creations."[15]

After nearly 35 years of serious collecting, Spingarn estimated his holdings by Black authors to include 2,700 books and pamphlets (nearly everything produced by Black writers since 1900), 1,000 musical compositions, several hundred slave narratives and autobiographies, and numerous additional varieties of literary work.[16] With a donation in 1941 of several dozen exceptional items (books, pamphlets, manuscripts), he helped Yale University's library to launch the James Weldon Johnson Memorial Collection of Negro Arts and Letters.[17] In 1948, Howard University announced the acquisition of more than 5,000 items, from rare to recent, that had constituted the bulk of Spingarn's library. The university's president, Mordecai Johnson, joined him in speaking at the opening of the collection in Howard's Founders Library.[18] That collection and one donated earlier by Black theologian Jesse E. Moorland would be reorganized into the nationally noted and comprehensive Moorland-Spingarn Research Center. Despite donating so much of his library, Spingarn's bibliophilic interests continued, as did his trips abroad and visits to book collectors. In 1949, he became an incorporator of the newly formed Cambridge Bibliographical Society.

Spingarn had long sought to support Black artists and writers early in their careers. With his reviews in the *Crisis* and his collecting reputation, he increasingly became a target for writers seeking editorial advice, publishers, and/or readers. For example, Julious Hill wrote from Oklahoma: "I have some plays for which I would desire a producer or an agent, also a publisher for my manuscripts." An Illinois songwriter, Leon Harris, reminded Spingarn that "last fall I mailed to you a copy of my book of railroad song-poems, 'I'm a Railroad Man.' As you did not mention this book in your February *Crisis* article, I was wondering if you received the copy." And a Virginia attorney and aspiring poet, J. M. Harrison, told him about his "small book of poems, entitled 'Southern Sunbeams,' artistically arranged and printed on fine quality book paper. . . . Reasonably priced at $1.00. May I have the honor of your subscription?"[19] At the very least, Spingarn was courteous and encouraging in return, although most such correspondents sought more attention than he was able to give.

In other cases, Spingarn sensed real abilities among young literary hopefuls and reached out with advice and encouragement. One of those was a young Texas schoolteacher, J. Mason Brewer, who began writing to Arthur in 1936 about his dreams of published authorship. During their 20 years of correspondence, Brewer earned a PhD and published books with the University of Texas Press and others.[20] Well-established writers, such as historian

John Hope Franklin, also called on Arthur's generous expertise. In the 1967 preface to his third edition of *From Slavery to Freedom,* Franklin thanked Spingarn profusely for help in correcting "several serious errors."[21]

⚖

Spingarn kept in touch often with his sister-in-law Amy and his adult nieces and nephews. He even tried to convince Amy to serve on the NAACP budget committee. Although she refused that appointment, she remained on the NAACP board of directors for nearly 40 years.[22] Nephew Stephen was in Washington, DC, as an assistant general counsel at the Department of the Treasury. He had served as an officer in the army's Counter Intelligence Corps during the war years and later as administrative assistant to President Harry Truman and as a commissioner at the Federal Trade Commission. Nephew Edward served in the US Army in World War II and the Korean War, eventually becoming an economist with the International Monetary Fund. Honor Spingarn had married in 1937 and moved to St. Thomas, Virgin Islands, where she became well known for her paintings and textile designs. Her correspondence to "Uncle Arthur" throughout the next several decades sometimes included books by Caribbean authors she felt deserved his attention. Niece Hope wrote lengthy letters to Arthur after leaving New York in 1957 to marry and settle first in Bombay (Mumbai), India, and then in London. Amy Spingarn continued her painting and philanthropy, while also traveling overseas from time to time. She eventually found Troutbeck a financial and personal burden, and she began plans for selling the Amenia estate a dozen years after Joel Spingarn's death.[23]

Somehow, Spingarn also found time to continue with a number of his own legal clients outside of the NAACP. Historian and biographer Van Wyck Brooks, for example, kept him busy with tax issues that changed from year to year, depending on his book sales and publishing agreements. The Pulitzer Prize and National Book Award winner regularly sent friendly letters from Westport, Connecticut, and Carmel, California, about "this troublesome business of my various income taxes." He included general estimates of book contract income ranging from slim to substantial, as well as his own thoughts about possible deductions and exemptions.[24] Although he didn't consider himself a tax lawyer, Arthur politely responded to Brooks's needs.

⚖

Undoubtedly, leaders in the struggle for civil rights were buoyed by the huge NAACP growth during the war years, which brought membership to nearly a half million. The 1944 annual conference in Chicago was attended by 600 delegates from 42 states. Its closing event in Washington Park attracted a crowd of approximately 30,000.[25] Under Thurgood Marshall's leadership, the NAACP Legal Department had grown to seven paid professionals, including four young and busy full-time lawyers. The department's staff and the national committee were strained with reviewing and advising on the several hundred cases handled in the branches annually, as well as planning for key cases that could attack issues of discrimination and injustice nationally. Although President Roosevelt had not compiled a fully admirable record of pushing for racial equality, Arthur Spingarn urged the NAACP to retreat from its usual nonpartisanship and support the president for a fourth term in 1944. He viewed the New Deal as imperfect, Roosevelt's position on race issues as equivocal, and Truman as a questionable pick for vice president. However, he insisted that "the Democratic Party was all Negroes had."[26] Walter White and others agreed, determining that the NAACP would do nothing to hinder the election of the Roosevelt-Truman ticket.

When Roosevelt died just months into his fourth term, Spingarn was publicly magnanimous in his remembrance. Although he had not convinced Roosevelt to back a federal antilynching bill nor to end discrimination in the military, Spingarn emphasized the progress that had been made toward nondiscriminatory hiring in federal civilian jobs and contracts. In a radio speech, he proclaimed the president's death "a tragic loss to mankind and particularly to the minority groups in this country. . . . Few men in public life today have been more interested in their problems, more sympathetic with their handicaps, more aroused by their sufferings from injustices and discriminations."[27]

Although Spingarn had doubts about President Truman, those dissipated in the light of executive orders and other actions that demonstrated Truman's commitment to advancing racial justice. The new president quickly appointed the President's Committee on Civil Rights. With nearly half its members suggested by NAACP executive secretary Walter White, it was charged with investigating racial discrimination and civil rights conditions. In 1947, Truman addressed the closing session of the annual NAACP meeting, sharing a platform at the Lincoln Memorial with White and Eleanor Roosevelt. He spoke for a broad federal role in ending racial violence and supporting equal opportunity. When the President's Committee on Civil Rights released its report, *To Secure These Rights*, it "sparked a national discussion on civil rights, provided ammunition for civil rights legislation on Capitol Hill, and created a platform for President Truman."[28] Soon after, Truman addressed a joint session of the US Congress to call for federal antilynching legislation, voting rights protections, a new Fair Employment Practices Commission, and a Civil Rights Division in the US Department of Justice. He noted that the executive branch had already begun actions to improve enforcement of civil rights statutes and eliminate discrimination in federal employment and all areas of the armed services. Arthur Spingarn eventually summed up the postwar president as "very decent." And he found honesty in Truman's claim of harboring "no prejudice of any nature or description."[29] Spingarn was particularly pleased with his nephew Stephen's work in the Truman administration.

⚖️

Surprisingly, the postwar years also witnessed the return of W. E. B. Du Bois to the NAACP, a circumstance initially supported by Spingarn. When Atlanta University did not renew the contract of the 75-year-old Du Bois in 1943, Spingarn noted that Du Bois had worked there "against ignorance, bigotry, intolerance and slothfulness, projecting ideas nobody but he understands and raising hopes for change which may be comprehended in a hundred years."[30] Du Bois returned to New York to serve as NAACP director of special research for several years, but he never resolved his earlier differences with Walter White. Du Bois's ideas about labor and economic issues now seemed to lean beyond even his earlier Marxism toward embracing communism. After Du Bois's final NAACP departure, Spingarn was invited to serve as honorary chair of a committee celebrating his 83rd birthday. Although Spingarn had attended his old colleague's 80th birthday celebration, he had grown increasingly distant from him. Now he responded that while he viewed Du Bois as a "great man," he found that Du Bois's positions in recent years "differ so radically from my own on fundamental political issues that I must regretfully decline to accept the invitation." Later, after Du Bois's death in 1963, Spingarn fumed that Du Bois had indeed been a communist—still a "great man" but one who "went sour." Yet at a testimonial dinner two years later, Spingarn insisted that although he disapproved of many of Du Bois's actions, he still viewed him as "one of the truly great figures of the twentieth century."[31]

⚖️

On May 17, 1954, Arthur Spingarn sat smiling between Walter White and Thurgood Marshall while various NAACP leaders addressed the press and scores of interested citizens at the association's Manhattan headquarters on West 40th Street. The unanimous Supreme Court decision in *Brown v. Board of Education* had been announced earlier that day, perhaps the most stunning legal victory in NAACP history. Jack Greenberg, who served as co-counsel with Marshall on the case, later recalled: "After every other Supreme Court victory we had celebrated with a raucous, boozy party. But after *Brown*, there was quiet. It was all so awesome. We still didn't know what it meant or where it would lead."[32]

Marshall, who had brought together several cases for Supreme Court consideration in making the argument for the end of school segregation, knew that implementation would be slow—perhaps "up to five years" for the entire country. He noted to the press that the association had already begun to train lawyers throughout the country to grapple with local violations of compliance.[33] Fully believing that defiant white citizens and political leaders, particularly in the South, would not comply without many years of struggle, Spingarn was more pessimistic about the time frame for true school desegregation. At best, he hoped it might be completed by the 1963 centennial of the Emancipation Proclamation. His presidential address at the July 1954 annual NAACP meeting was congratulatory and upbeat, but he warned of the need for continued pressure:

> We should all feel gratified that it was the NAACP with its guiding hand and the bitterly hard work of Thurgood Marshall and his associates that were responsible for this great victory. At the same time that we rejoice in this overwhelming victory for democracy, we must already turn our thoughts to the future and to the work which remains to be done to achieve full freedom for American Negro citizens. Ahead of us during the next nine years are many, many hours of work and of planning for more work and even some temporary set-backs before we reach our emancipation centennial goal.... The forces of reaction in the United States are many and will be heard. But the forces for democracy are great and growing. Let us resolve not to be deterred.[34]

While several hundred school districts desegregated during the year following the Supreme Court ruling, white political leaders in the Deep South remained adamant that their schools would stay segregated. Even after a 1955 Supreme Court decree calling for all districts to move promptly toward compliance, little changed. Sullivan notes that "national political leadership collapsed in the face of southern defiance. President [Dwight] Eisenhower never publicly endorsed *Brown*, and he privately opposed it."[35] Southern states found various ways to interrupt NAACP chapter activities and to continue discrimination. Nevertheless, Black citizens began organizing at the community, state, and finally national levels to push for equal rights in a va-

President Dwight D. Eisenhower greets NAACP officials, including Arthur Spingarn (*third from left*). Photograph by Fred Harris, William Hastie Photographs, courtesy of Historical & Special Collections, Harvard Law School Library

riety of situations. The example of Rosa Parks and the Montgomery bus boycott was followed by Freedom Riders, protest marches, and sit-ins well into the 1960s. Eventually, the 1964 Civil Rights Act and the 1965 Voting Rights Act would be passed by the US Congress and signed into law by President Lyndon Johnson.

⚖

Arthur Spingarn greatly curtailed his active involvement with the NAACP shortly after the *Brown* decision. However, journalist James Ivy described him at age 78 as still "a forceful and resourceful man . . . a fluent and graceful talker of vivacity and charm."[36] When Arthur's wife, Marion, died in 1958, she had been an invalid for several years, a condition Arthur determined was the result of her many years of 18-hour days as a social worker dedicated to bettering lives.[37] He continued to live in their Gramercy Park home, with many books and much artwork. Among his active membership groups were the New York Tuberculosis and Health Association, the New York State Commission against Discrimination, the Association for the Study of Negro Life and History, and the New York Public Library. He traveled to Nigeria in 1960 for that country's celebration of its newly independent status and freedom from British rule. Undoubtedly well aware of the important historic issues and events that had marked the years of his adult life, in 1962 he began sorting through his personal papers and sending them to the Library of Congress.

As he followed events related to US race relations in the 1960s and early 1970s, Spingarn was both hopeful and conflicted. Strong opinions and mass actions contrasted with decades of the NAACP's more selective approaches. Representative Adam Clayton Powell Jr. of Harlem criticized the association's inclusion of many white leaders and viewed its legal moves through the courts as "nit-picking."[38] When NAACP executive secretary Roy Wilkins, the Reverend Martin Luther King Jr., and others had announced a 1963 march on the nation's capital to support civil rights legislation, Spingarn had stated he had "serious doubts on the wisdom of the march . . . as to how it would affect these Republican senators."[39] However, he later clarified that his doubts were not related to potential violence: "after all, you cannot make an omelet without breaking eggs." He soundly opposed the Black Muslim advocacy of a separate state, and he voiced little patience for the Black Power movement's turn away from integration. Somewhat skeptical about the "demagoguery" of King, he was truly exasperated by the militancy of Stokely Carmichael and Malcolm X. He admired some of the new nonviolent groups and leaders, such as James Farmer at the Congress of Racial Equality. He stated: "None of this is new to me or the NAACP. We may not be running the Freedom Riders, but we've been trying their cases all along, for once they land in jail they turn to us."[40] At the same time, he was encouraged to see more Black leadership in the cause of Black justice:

> Fifty years ago Negroes wanted their rights as a woman wants a mink coat. Now they're ready to die for them. Today a leader has to be militant and willing to suffer or he's out. . . . I wish they were better organized, but I can't blame them. After all, they've been waiting for almost one hundred years for what they're legally entitled to.[41]

As someone who met all the US presidents during his years with the NAACP, Spingarn had strong opinions about their personal styles and their contributions to race relations. He had been pleased with the racial justice stance maintained by President Truman. Yet he had found President Eisenhower, whom he met four times, "a very likeable man but a man of very low intelligence." In contrast, he decided that President John F. Kennedy, who often had asked him to join discussions when African dignitaries visited, "had brains, really had brains." Spingarn happily recalled that "when Kennedy invited you for lunch, he not only gave you a swell dinner, but he gave you wines ... a Montrachet 1942 with every course. FDR invited you to lunch and you might get frankfurters." He was particularly proud that Kennedy once had introduced him at a public dinner as "an old and valued friend." By 1966 he determined that President Johnson, although "very vain" and "dogmatic," had "done some fine things, and he's done more for the Negro than any other president and at great sacrifice. Many of the southern states voted Republican just on that account."[42]

In early 1966, at age 87, Spingarn announced his retirement from the presidency of the NAACP, explaining that it was time for "a younger, more vigorous" leader. For the first time since 1911, neither Spingarn brother was an officer of the organization. In announcing his departure, the *Crisis* noted that he was still "hale and hearty" with a "deep sense of humor and a rapier-like wit." Spingarn retained his membership on the 60-person NAACP board of directors.[43] He also continued for several years to compile lists of books by Black authors for the *Crisis*.

Shortly after his NAACP retirement, Spingarn spoke frankly and at length in interviews for the Oral History Research Office at Columbia University. He was determined to clarify his position on skin color as a defining identity: "I haven't said this publicly. . . . This 'white' and 'negro' is a ridiculous thing. You and I are not white. A great many of those negroes, like Walter White, are blonds. I like to call them Europeans and Africans. So many of these Negroes now making a fuss are biologically European, not African."[44]

After a lengthy illness, Arthur Spingarn died at age 93 on December 1, 1971. He was survived by his brother Sigmund, his sister-in-law Amy, and his nieces and nephews. At Spingarn's memorial service, which was attended by equal numbers of Black and white mourners, Roy Wilkins declared: "The young people—both black and white—profess that the civil rights movement began in 1960 and that nothing ever happened before that." However, he reminded the attendees, Spingarn had made the "first assault" on racial discrimination in 1910. US Supreme Court associate justice Thurgood Marshall concluded his stirring eulogy with a simple assertion: "If it had not been for Arthur Spingarn, we would not have an NAACP today."[45]

Beyond Brotherhood

When Joel Spingarn included in his will a trust to ensure the continuance of the annual Spingarn Medal, he explained his desire "to perpetuate the life-long interest of my brother, Arthur B. Spingarn, of my wife, Amy E. Spingarn, and myself in the achievements of the American Negro."[1] It is not surprising that Arthur was prominent in Joel's thoughts. Yet, both Spingarns were defined by much more than the brotherly bond that connected them in many early experiences and later endeavors. While they grew up with similar enjoyments, such as reading good literature and inventing their own youthful stories, their differences in demeanor and in their preferred activities became striking. However, those disparities also served to highlight the commitment they most closely shared and that shaped their legacies: the ongoing struggle for racial equality.

Nothing of the brothers' early lives foretold their eventual work in developing and shaping the NAACP. Their family history had no tradition of abolitionist interests or even any well-defined political leanings. As they matured toward higher education and professional choices, the Spingarns seemed to share less common ground than in their boyhood years. Joel, while busily interested in personalities and events, honed his love of literature into masterful teaching and writing, including poetry and literary criticism. Arthur, more patient and watchful, enjoyed both the intricacies and the demands of legal work. Even as their mutual race-related concerns coincided and grew, the two maintained separate and diverse interests outside their NAACP leadership. Arthur had his consuming work in collecting, trading, and selling books and other publications; in heralding Black literary achievements in print and in speeches; and in pursuing his legal practice. His travels overseas were frequent and extensive, especially to Europe, Africa, and Caribbean nations. Additionally, his interest and expertise in social hygiene encouraged him to research, write, and lobby about curbing problems that ranged from inner cities to military camps. Joel had his literary pursuits as both a poet and essayist and, with Harcourt, Brace, as a publisher. His political interests led to a run for the US Congress and service as a delegate to national conventions. He was immersed in family life with his wife, Amy, and their sons and daughters, as well as in civic and social endeavors near his country estate in Amenia. There, he also developed a botanical expertise that stretched far and wide as he published journal articles and entertained visiting botanists. Both brothers served their country in World War I, although in different capacities.

The brothers also seemed endowed with very different outward personalities. Although both could be viewed as favoring activism, their approaches were not the same. Where Joel chose confrontation, Arthur chose compromise. The youngster who ran away to Philadelphia was ready for immediate action. The preteen who had begun to collect and sell rare books was comfortable with studied progress. Du Bois biographer David Levering Lewis describes Arthur as more warm and personable than his erudite older brother, who had "intense fire and flair."[2] The tribute to Joel in the *Crisis* just after his death concluded: "In discussions of policy and procedure, Colonel Spingarn could always be counted on to take the militant and uncompromising position. Upon matters of principle, he was adamant, preferring at all times to be right rather than safe."[3] Joel could often alienate even the friends of the struggle for racial justice. However, the NAACP proved to be a place that benefited from his strident insistence in areas he favored. And it also benefited from Arthur's patience for long-term gain as he watched and waited for just the right court case opportunities. The brothers' mutual interest in promoting racial justice undoubtedly helped to overcome their differences in professional choices and personal styles.

Since they were concerned with numerous long-term structural and systemic inequities that continue to avoid full resolution, Arthur and Joel could be viewed merely as placeholders in an ongoing struggle. However, several essential legal victories began under Arthur's oversight, demonstrating the importance of carefully selected and crafted cases that could extend the reach of civil rights and equal opportunity. Widespread attention to racial realities grew significantly with Joel's national outreach and political lobbying, prompting remarkable growth in the organization's branches, membership, and financial resources. The conferences he hosted at Troutbeck gave voice to diverse approaches and highlighted common goals.

During the time of the Spingarns' work, the overarching goal was to move racial equity beyond "separate but equal," even if that might mean separate *and* equal. Although decades later a slow and studied approach might seem compromising, the concept allowed some necessary contributions toward equity in education, residential circumstances, employment, and other key facets of opportunity. The brothers' early achievements for their cause were undoubtedly far more incremental than immediate. Yet their efforts often demonstrated possibilities that attracted others to their work and paved the way for continuing change. Closer to home, their discovery of shared interests and emotions regarding racial realities extended their relationship beyond loving siblings to partners in a true brotherhood.

⚖

The influence of the Spingarns' Jewish heritage on their work for racial justice was likely less prominent than it might have been in other times or places. Their circumstances and activities, stemming from their parents' immigration prior to the Civil War, were largely embedded in ideas about community, national origin, and integration with their immediate surroundings. They adhered to a reform style of Judaism and had no interest in Zionism. Yet their heritage pointed them toward a community that shared a commitment to fairness and equity for all—a sense of caring reflected in the important traditions of philanthropy among Jews. The Spingarns' Jewish background surfaced somewhat more in their family ties. For example, in autobiographical notes, Joel wrote a list of their mother's married siblings and their locations, carefully noting in each case whether their spouses were Jewish or gentile.[4]

Analysts have suggested that the substantial early Jewish interest in race issues was at least somewhat related to kindred identification. Certainly, the contributions of Jewish supporters were important in efforts for Black rights throughout the late nineteenth and early twentieth centuries. However, historian Gerald Sorin reminds us of a wider view:

> In the first place, Jewish culture was not monolithic. All immigrant groups, including the Jews, were divided by varying combinations of geographical origin, class, dialect, politics, and degree of adherence to traditional religion....
> In an ever changing American context, the children and grandchildren of Jewish immigrants tied to capitalism and urbanization, but simultaneously

tied to their Jewish traditions, households, and community, constructed over time an American Jewish ethnic identity.[5]

As discrimination against Jews grew in the late nineteenth century, at about the same time that the end of Reconstruction ushered in renewed bigotry toward Black citizens, some shared feelings about this expanded prejudice were perhaps inevitable. And some were undoubtedly deeply rooted in Jewish spiritual and scriptural precepts related to one's duty toward others. The Spingarns' friend and associate W. E. B. Du Bois proclaimed in 1923 that "the Negro race looks to Jews for sympathy and understanding."[6] Yet there is no evidence that the brothers themselves ever contemplated a direct connection between elements of their Jewish heritage and their recognition of the Black experience. Instead, Joel's early indignation at reported violence against southern Black sharecroppers seemed rooted in his natural inclinations toward justice for all. Arthur's commitment to legal resolution began with his firsthand outrage when handling a 1905 civil rights case. Thirty years later, noted lawyer Arthur Garfield Hays recalled Arthur's ongoing "remarkable capacity for indignation for the wrongs of others."[7] Whatever the source of the brothers' motivations, their determination was shared by many non-Jewish white colleagues—such as Mary White Ovington, Oswald Garrison Villard, and Charles Studin—who also saw wrongs and sought change.

While the Spingarns' Jewish heritage was likely at play—through community interactions or family role modeling—in shaping their interests in issues of racial inequality, their positions of financial well-being also contributed. This was especially true of Joel, whose resources increased greatly with marriage, providing comfortable travel, a palatial country estate, and a large city home complete with an elevator. The Spingarns' work toward improvements for Black citizens fit the political science concept of "noneconomic liberalism." Historian B. Joyce Ross defines the term as "strong reformist impulses in the realms of civil liberties, race relations, and foreign affairs but not in the basic distribution of wealth and power."[8] Social and political advancement is one thing, but economic empowerment is quite another. Among the very wealthy, including numerous early NAACP leaders, these tenets came so naturally as to indicate little or no deliberate motivation. The purposes and programs they designed concerned civil and political rights. These proponents believed that once those rights were secured, Black citizens could freely and fairly manage their own economic betterment. Although the early rich white activists eventually were willing to consider some limited NAACP attention to economic equality, they were especially reluctant to embrace what they saw as labor movement extremes. Only much later would noneconomic liberalism receive any serious challenge from within and outside the NAACP.

ΌΌ

While their noneconomic liberalism may have guided the Spingarns' approaches to addressing racial issues, their own economic well-being contributed to their personal support of efforts and individuals aiming for a better future. By funding the Spingarn Medal for outstanding Black achievement, Joel ensured ongoing recognition of Black accomplishments in a variety of fields. The first annual medal was awarded in 1915 to noted biologist Ernest Just. Awardees for literary accomplishments have included Charles Chesnutt, Richard Wright, and Alex Haley. Educators Mary McLeod Bethune and John Hope, as well as vocal artists Leontyne Price, Marian Anderson, and Lena Horne, have been honored with the medal. Twenty-first-century winners have included Julian Bond, Oprah Winfrey, Sidney Poitier, John Lewis, and James Clyburn.

Joel and Amy Spingarn are remembered in Amenia for their early pioneering work that addressed Dutchess County community concerns. Their estate, Troutbeck, became a conference center for a while in the late twentieth century, but was nearly abandoned in the early twenty-first century. Restored and renovated in 2017, it is now a sprawling country hotel with first-class accommodations, fine dining, spas, swimming pools, tennis courts, and bike trails. Copies of a note from Dr. Martin Luther King Jr. to Amy Spingarn hang in every guest room, and a hotel placard reads "Troutbeck, Amenia, NY. Hosting writers, environmentalists and civil rights leaders since 1765."[9] The 1830 Federal-style home of Spingarn friend Lewis Mumford, just down the road from Troutbeck, was placed on the National Register of Historic Places in 1999.

Arthur's lifelong effort to collect and promote literature, poetry, musical scores, and other works by Black artists is now best accessed at the Moorland-Spingarn Research Center at Howard University. Thousands of books and other items from Arthur's personal library have been combined with materials from Black theologian Jesse E. Moorland to create one of the world's largest collections documenting the Black experience. The collection showcases Black achievements and hosts hundreds of researchers each year. Arthur also sent duplicates and smaller collections to Yale University and the University of California, Los Angeles. His will, which provided a testamentary trust for several relatives during their lifetimes, reverted on their deaths to the Arthur B. Spingarn Memorial Scholarship Fund at Columbia University, which was started in 1992 with $500,000.[10]

While the Spingarn name still labels a medal, a high school, a scholarship, and archival collections, the remembrance of Joel and Arthur has faded. That they became less and less remarked over time is not entirely surprising. Their efforts and achievements for racial equity were tireless but widely scattered—developing essential court cases, lobbying government officials, gaining Black military officer participation, integrating public spaces, expanding the NAACP's reach, and beyond. And they each became identified with numerous interests and endeavors beyond their race-related work. Therefore, they were never easily linked to notable and readily recognized accomplishments or ideas, such as Frederick Douglass's struggle for abolition, Booker T. Washington's commitment to economic bootstrapping, or Thurgood Marshall's success in school desegregation.

Additionally, the methods and means the Spingarn brothers and their colleagues initially brought to the struggles for Black citizens soon took a back seat to more impatient activism. Boycotts, marches, sit-ins, mass demonstrations, and slogans began an era of civil disobedience that won attention and some eventual success. Historian Kenneth Janken aptly notes of that period: "Generation and politics divided the new wave of activists from the civil rights establishment. . . . They drew inspiration from Gandhi, Niebuhr, and, somewhat later, Malcolm X and African independence struggles."[11] Earlier civil rights endeavors—including celebratory speeches, legal battles, appeals to public officials, and print journalism—began to seem limited and even outmoded. Their proponents gradually receded in memory. Yet in advancing the ideal of racial equality to the status of national attention, Joel and Arthur Spingarn were crucial to identifying Black people's needs, arousing support, and achieving early victories. They nurtured a cause that later became a movement.

ACKNOWLEDGMENTS

Encouragement, support, and assistance were essential in completing this volume. As my research and writing slowly proceeded during the COVID-19 pandemic, the individuals who provided those elements became even more crucial. They ranged from caring friends to scholarly reviewers and from graduate assistants to professional archivists—and beyond.

The first person to offer the interest necessary to undertake the project was Johns Hopkins University Press acquisitions editor Laura Davulis. Her reassurance was particularly important as my progress slowed during the closing of libraries and collections due to the spread of COVID-19. Assistant acquisitions editor Ezra Rodriguez was helpful in providing guidelines and responding to my changing estimates of manuscript delivery, while managing editor Juliana McCarthy oversaw my final manuscript through to publication. During the earliest planning stages of this project, a number of academic colleagues shared valuable insights concerning historical and organizational issues. These generous individuals included Professors Christian Anderson, John Thelin, Jon Tuttle, Robert Luke, Barbara Tobolowsky, and Iris Saltiel. Judy Harris and Philip Kaplan provided essential information on ideas and meanings related to Jewish heritage and practices.

I was fortunate to have the research assistance of two very savvy and persistent individuals who were completing graduate school at the time: Cappy Yarbrough and Jackson Palmour. I greatly benefited from their ability to arrange online access to necessary materials held in collections that were closed to in-person research. Mary Grimes-McGreer, the photo editor for the manuscript, managed to locate possible sources and gain access to images; and Diane Sarrocco produced the index. John S. McCormack provided early editorial assistance by examining the initial drafts of each chapter for clarity and consistency of expression. Finally, copyeditor Merryl Sloane brought her expertise and patience to the final draft, identifying not only errors but also opportunities to produce a far better final book.

In person and online, my research greatly depended on the guidance and good graces of librarians and archivists at various collections that held personal papers and background information that could help me understand and explain the lives of the Spingarn brothers. At the Moorland-Spingarn Research Center at Howard University, I was especially fortunate in the assistance of archivist Sonja Woods. Likewise, Meredith Mann, Tal Nadan, and others supported my searches in the Manuscripts and Archives Division of the New York Public Library, as did Stephen Simon, the curator of Special Collections at the New York Botanical Garden. I also benefited from generous and knowledgeable professionals at the Library of Congress's Manuscript Division, Yale University's Beinecke Rare Book and Manuscript Library, the Library of the University of Massachusetts at Amherst, and the Columbia University Oral History Research Office. My "home" libraries at the University of South Carolina and the College of Charleston provided numerous volumes necessary for my understanding of various historical contexts and events.

Valuable feedback on draft segments along the way came from fellow writers Carol Mason, Jo Ana Finger, Robert Morris, Doc Ardrey, Mary Eaddy, and Ginny Foard. Other friends and family who kept the project going through their expressions of frequent interest and encouragement included Roger Akin, Wallace Winter, Emilie Egan, Alicia Caudill, Judy Wolk, Joan Marchetti, Amber Stegelin, Vivian Derienzo, Laura McMaster, Bob Toy, and Cathy Maddaloni. As always, my most heartfelt gratitude goes to my daughter and son, Adrienne Reynolds Cohen and Brett Reynolds, and to their spouses, Bret Cohen and Britt Haxton. A final word of appreciation is due to a tabby cat named Squeeze, who faithfully accompanied me on long days of writing by sleeping on a corner of my desk.

Abbreviations

ABS	Arthur Barnett Spingarn
BRBML-JES	Joel E. Spingarn Collection, Beinecke Rare Book and Manuscript Library, Yale University, New Haven, CT
BRBML-WDB	W. E. B. Du Bois Collection, Beinecke Rare Book and Manuscript Library, Yale University, New Haven, CT
CUOHRO	Columbia University Oral History Research Office, New York
JES	Joel Elias Spingarn
LOC-ABS	Arthur B. Spingarn Papers, Library of Congress, Washington, DC
LOC-NAACP	Records of the National Association for the Advancement of Colored People, Library of Congress, Washington, DC
MSRC-ABS	Arthur B. Spingarn Papers, Moorland-Spingarn Research Center, Howard University, Washington, DC
MSRC-JES	Joel E. Spingarn Papers, Moorland-Spingarn Research Center, Howard University, Washington, DC
NYBG-JES	Joel E. Spingarn Papers, Archives and Manuscripts, Mertz Library, New York Botanical Garden
NYPL-JES	Joel E. Spingarn Papers, Manuscript and Archives Division, New York Public Library
NYPL-JSAS	Joel E. and Amy E. Spingarn Papers, Manuscript and Archives Division, New York Public Library
SCMA-WDB	W. E. B. Du Bois Papers, Special Collections and University Archives, University of Massachusetts, Amherst

Introduction • Brothers and Brotherhood

1. Martin Austermuhle, "Exploring a Huge Abandoned DC High School," https://www.youtube.com/watch?v=gOGllSheVMM.

2. Rosenthal, *Nicholas Miraculous,* 211.

3. Cheryl Greenberg, "Negotiating Coalition: Black and Jewish Civil Rights Agencies," in Salzman and West, *Struggles in the Promised Land,* 143–73.

4. David Levering Lewis, "Shortcuts to the Mainstream: Afro-American and Jewish Notables in the 1920s and 1930s," in Washington, *Jews in Black Perspectives,* 85.

5. Quoted in Dalin, *Jewish Justices*, 276.

6. Ross, *J. E. Spingarn*, 222.

7. "Reminiscences of Arthur Spingarn"; Gary, "White Warrior," 64.

Chapter 1 • Sons of Determination

1. JES, autobiographical notes, NYPL-JES. See also Van Deusen, *J. E. Spingarn*, 15.

2. Sorin, *Tradition Transformed*, 22.

3. JES, autobiographical notes, NYPL-JES.

4. Quoted in Mumford, Introduction, 74.

5. "Reminiscences of Arthur Spingarn," 12–13.

6. JES, autobiographical notes, NYPL-JES.

7. "Reminiscences of Arthur Spingarn," 69; Ross, *J. E. Spingarn*, 4.

8. JES, autobiographical notes, NYPL-JES.

9. "Lost to Home and College," *Evening World* (New York), June 19, 1890; "City and Suburban News," *New York Times*, June 20, 1890.

10. JES to Elias Spingarn, June 21, 1890, NYPL-JES, Family Letters.

11. JES, autobiographical notes, NYPL-JES.

12. JES to Elias Spingarn, June 21, 1890.

13. "Reminiscences of Arthur Spingarn," 2–3.

14. JES, autobiographical notes, NYPL-JES.

15. JES to Sarah Barnett Spingarn, August 6, 8, 9, and 12, 1893, NYPL-JES, Family Letters.

Chapter 2 • The Columbia Stamp

1. Thompson, "Arthur Barnett Spingarn," 54.

2. "Reminiscences of Arthur Spingarn," 52.

3. "Reminiscences of Arthur Spingarn," 64–65.

4. Keppel *Columbia*, 80–81, 275–76.

5. Chaddock, *Multi-Talented Mr. Erskine*, 24–25.

6. Cane, *All and Sundry*, 103.

7. Erskine, *Memory*, 96.

8. "Reminiscences of Arthur Spingarn," 3–4; JES, "Literature and the New Era" (lecture at the New School for Social Research, February 18, 1931), quoted in Ross, *J. E. Spingarn*, 4.

9. JES, "George Edward Woodberry," 10:479–81. See also Hovey, "George Edward Woodberry," 512–14.

10. "Columbia Verse," *Columbia Spectator* 40, no. 28 (December 15, 1897): 2.

11. JES, "Lyly's 'Endimion,'" 172.

12. Hofstadter, *Anti-Intellectualism*, 408.

13. JES to Sarah B. Spingarn, September 30, 1895, NYPL-JES, Family Letters.

14. Quoted in "Oral History Interview with Stephen J. Spingarn," 3.

15. Erskine, *Memory*, 103.

16. Sinclair, *Goose-Step*, 13; Lewisohn, *Upstream*, 107–8.

17. Van Deusen, *J. E. Spingarn*, 18.

18. McCaughey, *Stand, Columbia*, 183–85.

19. JES, "Politics and the Poet," 75.

20. Ross, *J. E. Spingarn*, 5.

Chapter 3 • No Simple Launch

1. "Reminiscences of Arthur Spingarn," 5.

2. Van Deusen, *J. E. Spingarn*, 180; "Commencement at Columbia," *New York Times*, May 25, 1901.

3. Ross, *J. E. Spingarn*, 11.

4. JES to ABS, August 7, 1902, NYPL-JES, Family Letters.

5. JES to ABS, August 13 and 19, 1902, NYPL-JES, Family Letters; Mutzenberg, *Kentucky's Famous Feuds*, 282–99.

6. JES to ABS, August 29, 1902, NYPL-JES, Family Letters.

7. "Comparative Literature," *New York Times*, February 2, 1903.

8. Robert M. Gay, "Atlantic Repartee," typescript, November 8, 1942, NYPL-JES, Personal-Miscellaneous.

9. Lewis, "Mumford and the Academy," 103.

10. Knopf, "Columbia I Remember," 183.

11. George E. Woodberry to JES, January 14, 1904, quoted in Rosenthal, *Nicholas Miraculous*, 153.

12. "Criticizes Butler and Quits Columbia," *New York Times*, February 4, 1904.

13. JES to Sarah B. Spingarn, June 26, 1908, NYPL-JES, Family Letters.

14. "Reminiscences of Arthur Spingarn," 55.

15. "Oral History Interview with Stephen J. Spingarn," 8.

16. "Prominent Men Endorse Professor Spingarn," *Columbia Spectator* 52, no. 25 (October 21, 1908); "Roosevelt for Spingarn," *New York Times*, October 20, 1908.

17. JES to George Edward Woodberry, November 18, 1908, quoted in Van Deusen, *J. E. Spingarn*, 24.

18. "Oral History Interview with Stephen J. Spingarn," 3–4.

19. JES to Woodberry, November 18, 1908, 24.

20. "The Professor in Politics," *Columbia Spectator* 52, no. 4 (January 27, 1909): 1.

21. John Burroughs, Introduction, in Benton, *Troutbeck*, 4.

22. Du Bois, *Amenia Conference*, 3–4.

Chapter 4 • Roots of Activism

1. Sullivan, *Lift Every Voice*, 18; "The Pink Franklin Case," *Crisis* 1 (November 1910): 14.

2. William C. Hine, "Pink Franklin: NAACP'S First Legal Case," *Times and Democrat* (Orangeburg, SC), May 18, 2014.

3. Hine, "Pink Franklin"; Frances Blascoer to Pink Franklin, December 24, 1910, LOC-NAACP; Moorfield Storey to ABS, October 9, 1919, LOC-NAACP, box 1:A19.

4. Meier, *Negro Thought*, 164; Meier and Rudwick, *Along the Color Line*, 81–82; Broussard, *African-American Odyssey*, 142. See also Morris, *Theodore Rex*, 467.

5. Du Bois, "Steve Greene's Story," 14; Giddings, "Missing in Action," 1–17; "Negro Has Been Spirited Away," *Forrest City Times* (AR), October 28, 1910; Kellogg, *NAACP*, 62–63.

6. Quoted in Ross, *J. E. Spingarn*, 20.

7. JES, "What the NAACP Expects of Its Youth," address, NAACP Annual Conference, Detroit, MI, July 1, 1937, Speeches and Press Clippings, NYPL-JES.

8. "West Side Race Riot," *New York Tribune*, August 16, 1900.

9. NAACP Board of Directors, "Salutation and Appreciation for Arthur B. Spingarn," January 20, 1966, typescript, MSRC-ABS.

10. Sacks, *Before Harlem*, 43.

11. Sacks, *Before Harlem*, 46.

12. Johnson, *Along This Way*, 170–224.

13. "New York Republicans Pass Resolutions for Innocent Soldiers," *New York Tribune*, March 20, 1908.

14. Broussard, *African-American Odyssey*, 139–44.

15. Du Bois, "Strivings of the Negro People," 134; Du Bois, "Of the Training of Black Men," 289–97.

16. Du Bois, "Relation of the Negroes," 121–40.

17. Du Bois, *Souls of Black Folk*; "The Negro Question," *New York Times*, April 25, 1903, 6; "Books People Are Reading," *New York Tribune*, August 17, 1903, 10; "Books and Authors," *New York Daily Tribune*, April 18, 1903, 10.

18. August Meier, "Booker T. Washington and the Rise of the NAACP," in Meier and Rudwick, *Along the Color Line*, 80.

19. Meier, "Booker T. Washington," 81–84.

20. Du Bois, *Dusk of Dawn*, 88–89; Rudwick, "Niagara Movement," 177–97.

21. Du Bois, *Dusk of Dawn*, 94–95.

22. Sullivan, *Lift Every Voice*, 3.

23. Sullivan, *Lift Every Voice*, 6.

24. Ovington, *Black and White*, 56.

25. Ovington, *Black and White*, 57; Kellogg, *NAACP*, 297–99.

26. Du Bois, *Autobiography*, 254.

27. Walling to Du Bois, June 8, 1910, and Du Bois to Walling, June 13, 1910, in Aptheker, *Correspondence*, 1:169–70.

28. Du Bois to JES, November 29, 1910, box 1, BRBML-WDB.

29. Kellogg, *NAACP*, 64–65; Oswald Garrison Villard to JES, n.d., MSRC-JES. See also "Men of the Month," *Crisis* 2, no. 4 (August 1911): 147; Ovington, "National Association for the Advancement of Colored People," 112.

30. Ross, *J. E. Spingarn*, 13; Jessie Fauset to JES, February 12, 1913, MSRC-JES.

31. Quoted in Harrison-Kahan, "Scholars and Knights," 69.

32. Diner, *In the Almost Promised Land*, 122.

33. Lewis, "Parallels and Divergences," 547–48.

34. Lewis, "Parallels and Divergences," 546.

35. JES to Woodberry, September 5, 1900, quoted in Van Deusen, *J. E. Spingarn*, 27.

36. Carle, "Race, Class, and Legal Ethics," 104.

37. Lewis, *W. E. B. Du Bois*, 488.

38. Bender, "Reflections," 65.

Chapter 5 • Goodbye, Columbia

1. Ross, *J. E. Spingarn*, 7.

2. JES, *Question of Academic Freedom*, 10.

3. JES to William Howard Taft, 1913, NYPL-JES.

4. Rosenthal, *Nicholas Miraculous*, 211.

5. Quoted in Rosenthal, *Nicholas Miraculous*, 334.

6. Klingenstein, *Jews in the American Academy*, 102.

7. Keppel to Butler, July 19, 1910, quoted in McCaughey, *Stand, Columbia*, 262.

8. Erskine, *My Life*, 107.

9. JES, *New Criticism*, 13.

10. JES, *New Criticism*, 20.

11. Erskine, *My Life*, 106.

12. JES to Isaac Goldberg, February 9, 1933, Isaac Goldberg Papers, New York Public Library.

13. JES, *Question of Academic Freedom*, 13.

14. JES, *Question of Academic Freedom*, 14.

15. "Letters of Professor Peck Figure in $50,000 Suit His 'Dear Tessie' Brings," *Evening World* (New York), June 1, 1910, 1.

16. Peck Clipping File, Rare Books and Manuscripts, Butler Library, Columbia University, New York.

17. Nicholas M. Butler Papers, University Archives, Butler Library, Columbia University, New York.

18. Rosenthal, *Nicholas Miraculous*, 204–6.

19. JES, *Question of Academic Freedom*, 18.

20. Erskine, *My Life*, 108–9.

21. JES to Butler, February 8, 1911, quoted in JES, *Question of Academic Freedom*, 24.

22. Butler to JES, January 16, 1911, quoted in JES, *Question of Academic Freedom*, 15.

23. JES to Butler, January 30, 1911, quoted in JES, *Question of Academic Freedom*, 16.

24. JES, *Question of Academic Freedom*, 19.

25. JES, *Question of Academic Freedom*, 20.

26. Columbia University Trustee Minutes, March 6, 1911, University Archives, Butler Library, Columbia University, New York.

27. Clements, *Art of Prestige*, 23.

28. Lewis, "Mumford and the Academy," 104.

29. "Professor Spingarn Out: Arraigns Dr. Butler," *New York Times*, March 10, 1911, 6.

30. "President Butler Autocratic He Says," *New York Times*, July 9, 1910, 2.

31. "Insurgent Spirit in Columbia Faculty," *New York Times*, May 14, 1911, 2.

32. Quoted in Sinclair, *Goose-Step*, 55.

33. Charles Beard, letter to *Columbia University Alumni News*, October 12, 1917, 59.

34. Sinclair, *Goose-Step*, 44.

35. Quoted in Rosenthal, *Nicholas Miraculous*, 216.

36. *Chicago Evening Post*, September 8, 1911, 9.

37. *Los Angeles Herald*, March 26, 1911, 12.

38. Quoted in *Sun* (New York), April 12, 1911, 9.

39. C. M. N., "New Hesperides," 508.

40. Quoted in Van Deusen, *J. E. Spingarn*, 65.

41. Harrison-Kahan, "Scholars and Knights," 69.

42. JES to Woodberry, May 7, 1911, quoted in Van Deusen, *J. E. Spingarn*, 54.

43. Woodberry to JES, n.d., quoted in JES, *Scholar's Testament*, 5.

Chapter 6 • *Joining by Doing*

1. "Men of the Month," *Crisis* 2, no. 4 (August 1911): 146; "Meeting," *Crisis* 3, no. 4 (February 1912): 158. See also Sullivan, *Lift Every Voice*, 19.

2. JES to ABS, April 7, 1913, LOC-ABS, reel 1.

3. Ross, *J. E. Spingarn*, 23.

4. "Meeting," 159.

5. "Meeting," 159.

6. "The New York Branch," *Crisis* 2, no. 4 (August 1911): 152–53.

7. "The N.A.A.C.P.," *Crisis* 2, no. 3 (August 1911): 60.

8. ABS, biographical notes, MSRC-ABS.

9. Kellogg, NAACP, 123; Ross, *J. E. Spingarn*, 22.

10. Ovington, *Black and White*, 69.

11. JES to Amy Spingarn, December 22, 1912, box 1, NYPL-JSAS.

12. Lewis, *W. E. B. Du Bois*, 487.

13. Quoted in Ross, *J. E. Spingarn*, 68–69.

14. Du Bois, *Autobiography*, 256.

15. Du Bois, *Autobiography*, 257.

16. Kellogg, NAACP, 149; Sullivan, *Lift Every Voice*, 22–24.

17. *Crisis* 5, no. 1 (November 1912): 30–31; *Crisis* 3, no. 1 (November 1911): 27–30.

18. Ovington, *Walls*, 108.

19. Du Bois, *Autobiography*, 256–57.

20. Du Bois to JES, October 23 and 28, 1914, box 1, BRBML-WDB.

21. JES to Du Bois, October 24, 1914, in Aptheker, *Correspondence*, 1:201.

22. Interview with Amy Spingarn, May 29, 1973, quoted in Thompson, "Arthur Barnett Spingarn," 60; Lewis, *W. E. B. Du Bois*, 475.

23. Du Bois, *Dusk of Dawn*, 255–56.

24. Brinsmade, "Our Legal Bureau," *Crisis* 8, no. 6 (April 1914): 291.

25. Hastie, "Toward an Egalitarian Legal Order," 21.

26. Meier and Rudwick, "Attorneys Black and White," 916. See also Woodson, *Negro Professional Man*.

27. Hughes, *Fight for Freedom*, 30.

28. Du Bois, *Autobiography*, 263.

29. Du Bois, *Autobiography*, 263.

30. JES to Amy Spingarn, August 4, 1912, MSRC-JES, Amy Spingarn Correspondence.

31. JES to Amy Spingarn, August 5, 1912, MSRC-JES, Amy Spingarn Correspondence.

32. "Name George Perkins N.Y. Committeeman," *Sun* (New York), August 7, 1912, 2.

33. Addams, "Progressive Party and the Negro," 30.

34. Du Bois, *Autobiography*, 263.

35. Quoted in Chace, *1912*, 163.

36. Theodore Roosevelt to Julian Harris, August 1, 1912, in Morison, *Letters of Theodore Roosevelt*, 7:107–11; Mowry, "South and the Progressive," 242.

37. Mumford, Introduction, 73.

38. "Oral History Interview with Stephen J. Spingarn," 5–6.

39. Sullivan, *Lift Every Voice*, 25–27; "Opinion," *Crisis* 5, no. 1 (November 1912): 18–22.

40. Cooper, *Reconsidering Woodrow Wilson*, 104–5.

41. Speech by Woodrow Wilson, July 29, 1913, quoted in Baker, *Woodrow Wilson*, 4:222.

42. "To the President," August 15, 1913, reprinted in *Crisis* 6, no. 6 (October 1913): 298–99.

43. Villard, *Fighting Years*, 240.

44. *Afro-American Ledger* (Baltimore, MD), April 5, 1913, quoted in Ross, *J. E. Spingarn*, 26.

45. Hughes, *Fight for Freedom*, 27.

46. Sullivan, *Lift Every Voice*, 25.

47. Stewart to JES, December 1, 1913, MSRC-JES.

48. JES to ABS, April 22, 1913; ABS to JES, July 10, 1913, and December 2, 1914, all in LOC-ABS, reel 1. See also Carle, "Race, Class, and Legal Ethics," 100–146.

49. ABS, *Laws Relating to Sex Morality*, xiii.

50. JES to ABS, October 15, 1915, LOC-ABS, reel 1.

51. ABS to Simon Adler, February 23, 1916, and ABS to Alfred Gilcrest, March 16, 1916, both in LOC-ABS, reel 1.

52. Typescript of paper presented at chapel exercises, n.d., MSRC-ABS.

53. ABS, "Collecting a Library," 16.

54. ABS, "Collecting a Library," 16.

55. "Rare Books," *New York Tribune*, April 28, 1917, 2. See also "Reminiscences of Arthur Spingarn."

56. "Closes Hearing on Einstein Will," *New York Times*, December 4, 1913, 9.

57. Mumford, "Scholar and Gentleman," 8.

58. Van Deusen, *J. E. Spingarn*, 59.

59. JES to Sterling Yard, July 13, 1914, NYPL-JES.

60. JES to ABS, October 5, 1915, LOC-ABS, reel 1.

61. Mary White Ovington, speech delivered at the NAACP Annual Conference, Cleveland, OH, quoted in Ross, *J. E. Spingarn*, 258; James Ivy, "Arthur Spingarn . . . Different Man to Different People," *Pittsburgh Courier*, May 12, 1956; Lewis, *W. E. B. Du Bois*, 473, 490; H. H. Zand, interview with Francis Thompson, quoted in Thompson, "Arthur Barnett Spingarn," 55.

62. Mumford, Introduction, 73; Lewis Einstein, unpublished reminiscence, quoted in Van Deusen, *J. E. Spingarn*, 23.

Chapter 7 • *New Tactics for New Abolition*

1. Carle, "Race, Class, and Legal Ethics," 122.

2. JES to ABS, December 16, 1914; JES to Amy Spingarn, December 31, 1914, both in LOC-ABS, reel 1.

3. Carle, "Race, Class, and Legal Ethics," 117.

4. ABS to H. Williamson, February 18, 1916, LOC-ABS, reel 2.

5. Minutes, NAACP Board of Directors, January 5, 1915, quoted in Sullivan, *Lift Every Voice*, 47.

6. ABS to JES, June 21, 1915, LOC-ABS, reel 1.

7. Du Bois, "Legal Work," 289.

8. Wright, "NAACP and Residential Segregation," 47.

9. Carle, "Race, Class, and Legal Ethics," 128.

10. See Barnett and Blackman, *Constitutional Law*.

11. Storey, in Board Minutes, NAACP, November 12, 1917, quoted in Wright, "NAACP and Residential Segregation," 51.

12. Hughes, *Fight for Freedom*, 27.

13. Sinclair to JES, January 4, 1915, MSRC-JES.

14. Ross, *J. E. Spingarn*, 27.

15. Sullivan, *Lift Every Voice*, 40.

16. Lewis, *W. E. B. Du Bois*, 485.

17. "Mr. Spingarn's Trips, 1914–1915," LOC-NAACP; Van Deusen, *J. E. Spingarn*, 163.

18. *New York Evening Post*, March 13, 1914, quoted in Ross, *J. E. Spingarn*, 30.

19. "Joel Spingarn Attacks Dr. Washington," *New York Age*, February 26, 1914.

20. "Sixth Annual Report," *Crisis* 11, no. 5 (March 1916): 255–56.

21. "Sees Argument for Suffrage in War," *New York Tribune*, December 4, 1914; "Suffrage Lawyers Talk This Week," *New York Tribune*, February 15, 1915.

22. "Wills and Appraisals," *Sun* (New York), October 1, 1914.

23. More than a hundred years later, after 200 failed attempts, an antilynching act passed both houses of the US Congress and was signed into law by President Joseph Biden in 2022.

24. ABS to May Childs Nerney, May 21, 1915, and C. T. Hallman to ABS, June 1, 1915, both in LOC-NAACP, box 1.

25. Du Bois, "Fighting Race Calumny," 40–42; Sullivan, *Lift Every Voice*, 47–50; JES, Report to the Board of Directors, January 3, 1916, LOC-NAACP, box 1.

26. "City Men Drive to Army Work," *New York Times*, August 11, 1915.

27. Van Deusen, *J. E. Spingarn*, 62–63; Ross, *J. E. Spingarn*, 83–84.

28. JES to ABS, January 11, 1916, LOC-ABS, reel 1.

29. ABS to Simon Adler, February 23, 1916, and Alfred Gilchrist to ABS, March 16, 1916, both in LOC-ABS, reel 1.

30. Johnson, *Along This Way*, 308.

31. Du Bois, *Dusk of Dawn*, 243.

32. Du Bois, *Amenia Conference*, 3.

33. ABS to JES, September 1916, NYPL-JES, Family Papers.

34. Du Bois, *Dusk of Dawn*, 245; Meier, *Negro Thought*, 184.

35. Johnson, *Along This Way*, 309; John Hope to JES, October 21, 1916, MSRC-JES.

36. Ovington to JES, December 20, 1915, NYPL-JES, Correspondence; Nerney to JES, January 6, 1916, MSRC-JES.

37. Johnson, *Along This Way*, 314–15.

38. Sullivan, *Lift Every Voice*, 64.

39. "Spingarn Estate," *New York Times*, April 1, 1919.

Chapter 8 • Great War, Great Debates

1. Ovington, *Walls*, 134.

2. Ovington to JES, July 2, 1917, MSRC-JES, Correspondence.

3. Du Bois, *Dusk of Dawn*, 249.

4. Quoted in Ellis, "W. E. B. Du Bois," 1586.

5. Du Bois, "Close Ranks," 93.

6. Wood to JES, January 9, 1917, MSRC-JES, Correspondence.

7. Quoted in "Training Camp Planned in Summer for Negroes," *Evening Star* (New York), February 23, 1917, 9.

8. J. M. Batchman, "No Segregation in Army Training School," *Chicago Defender*, March 3, 1917.

9. Ross, *J. E. Spingarn*, 91–93.

10. Kellogg, *NAACP*, 251–52; JES to Cook, May 2, 1917, MSRC-JES, Correspondence.

11. "The New Criticism," *New York Times*, July 1, 1917.

12. Quoted in Vitelli, *Van Wyck Brooks*, 74.

13. Nash to JES, May 7, 1917, BRBML-JES, box 1.

14. Du Bois, "Perpetual Dilemma," 171.

15. Ovington, *Walls*, 136.

16. Kennedy, *Over Here*, 158.

17. Johnson, *Along This Way*, 319.

18. Ovington, *Walls*, 135–39; Hughes, *Fight for Freedom*, 38–40. See also Sullivan, *Lift Every Voice*, 67–72.

19. War Department General Order 80, June 30, 1917, quoted in Ginn, *History*, 57.

20. "Reminiscences of Arthur Spingarn," 86.

21. "Reminiscences of Arthur Spingarn," 14.

22. ABS to JES, February 19, 1918, NYPL-JES, Family Papers.

23. "Reminiscences of Arthur Spingarn," 63–64; ABS, "War and Venereal Disease," 23.

24. ABS to JES, March 23, 1918, NYPL-JES, Family Papers; ABS to Secretary of State of New York, October 2, 1917, and ABS to Belle Davis, January 14, 1921, both in LOC-ABS, reel 1.

25. ABS to Amy Spingarn, October 21, 1918, NYPL-JES, Family Papers.

26. Thompson, "Arthur Barnett Spingarn," 54; "Man Shortage Causes Action," *Washington Herald*, September 16, 1918; "Seeks Women for the New Copette Force," *Washington Herald*, December 9, 1918.

27. Ovington to JES, July 5, 1917, MSRC-JES, Correspondence.

28. JES, "Complete Medical History," n.d., typescript, NYPL-JES, Personal-Miscellaneous.

29. JES to ABS, handwritten note on James Weldon Johnson to JES, November 25, 1917, LOC-ABS, reel 1.

30. "Spingarn Home Burns," *New York Times*, December 16, 1917.

31. Ross, *J. E. Spingarn*, 98.

32. JES, "The Sick Soldier," typescript, n.d., NYPL-JES, Personal-Miscellaneous.

33. ABS to Du Bois, July 3, 1918, SCMA-WDB; Du Bois, "Editorial," 215. See also Ross, *J. E. Spingarn*, 98–101.

34. JES to Du Bois, October 9, 1918, in Aptheker, *Correspondence*, 1:230.

35. JES to Hope Spingarn, November 23, 1918, MSRC-JES, Family Correspondence.

36. JES, "Sick Soldier," 8.

37. ABS to JES, December 2, 1918, NYPL-JES, Family Papers.

38. Aptheker, *Correspondence*, 230; Ovington, *Walls*, 169.

39. Ovington, *Walls*, 138–39; Jean Boileau, "The Negro Is Not without Honor," *Baltimore Evening Sun*, quoted in *Crisis* 19, no. 1 (November 1919): 344.

40. ABS to JES, April 10, 1919, NYPL-JES, Family Papers.

41. Du Bois to JES, January 15, 1919, BRBML-JES; JES to Du Bois, February 26, 1919, SCMA-WDB.

42. Du Bois, *Dusk of Dawn*, 262.

Chapter 9 • Aftermath

1. Johnson, *Along This Way*, 356–57.

2. Sullivan, *Lift Every Voice*, 91.

3. *Christian Science Monitor*, May 31, 1920, 4, quoted in Sullivan, *Lift Every Voice*, 92.

4. Kennedy, *Over Here*, 158.

5. Ovington, *Walls*, 147–51.

6. *Thirty Years of Lynching*, 2–3.

7. "Reminiscences of Arthur Spingarn."

8. "Urges Amendment to Bar Lynchings," *New York Times*, January 30, 1920, 10; Sullivan, *Lift Every Voice*, 105–9; Kennedy, *Over Here*, 283.

9. Du Bois, "Returning Soldiers," 14; Ovington, *Walls*, 169; Sullivan, *Lift Every Voice*, 86–87.

10. JES to Hope Spingarn, August 11, 1919, MSRC-JES, Family Correspondence.

11. Ross, *J. E. Spingarn*, 103–4; JES to James Weldon Johnson, June 27, 1921, LOC-NAACP, Administrative Files.

12. JES to Johnson, June 27, 1921.

13. Van Deusen, *J. E. Spingarn*, 66–68.

14. Elliott Rudwick and August Meier, "The Rise of the Black Secretariat in the NAACP, 1909–35," in Meier and Rudwick, *Along the Color Line*, 112–13; Sullivan, *Lift Every Voice*, 103–10.

15. Meier and Rudwick, "Attorneys Black and White," 915.

16. Du Bois, *Dusk of Dawn*, 239; Villard to ABS, January 31, 1924, LOC-ABS, reel 1.

17. Diner, *In the Almost Promised Land*, 125; White to ABS, October 28, 1928, LOC-ABS, reel 1.

18. David Levering Lewis, "Shortcuts to the Mainstream: Afro-American and Jewish Notables in the 1920s and 1930s," in Washington, *Jews in Black Perspectives*, 90.

19. Du Bois, "Brandeis," 243; Du Bois, "American Jew," 152.

20. "Reminiscences of Arthur Spingarn," 36; Rudwick and Meier, "Rise of the Black Secretariat," 114.

21. Du Bois to ABS, April 15, 1924, in Aptheker, *Correspondence*, 1:286.

22. "Reminiscences of Arthur Spingarn," 36.

23. Cobb to ABS, September 18, 1924, LOC-ABS, reel 1.

24. Sullivan, *Lift Every Voice*, 118–21.

25. ABS and White, memo, September 29, 1925, quoted in Janken, *White*, 75.

26. Quoted in White, *A Man Called White*, 75.

27. White to James Weldon Johnson, September 17, 1925, LOC-NAACP, Administrative Files.

28. Johnson, *Along This Way*, 384.

29. "N.A.A.C.P.," *Afro-American* (Baltimore, MD), October 23, 1926.

30. JES autobiographical notes, typescript, "Complete Medical History," NYPL-JES, Personal-Miscellaneous.

31. JES to Amy Spingarn, November 22, 1926, MSRC-JES, Family Correspondence.

32. ABS to White, March 6, 1928, MSRC-ABS, Correspondence.

33. Quoted in Mumford, Introduction, 74.

34. Mumford, Introduction, 74.

35. JES, autobiographical notes, NYPL-JES, quoted in Van Deusen, *J. E. Spingarn*, 66.

36. "In Brief Review," *Bookman*, February 1927, 753.

37. Brooks, *Days of the Phoenix*, 142; Hoopes, *Van Wyck Brooks*, 161–62.

38. Brooks, *Days of the Phoenix*, 161; JES to Hope Spingarn, July 30, 1928, NYPL-JES, Family Correspondence.

39. Ross, *J. E. Spingarn*, 118–19.

40. Ross, *J. E. Spingarn*, 117.

41. "The Amy Spingarn Prizes in Literature and Art," *Crisis* 29, no. 9 (November 1924): 24; "Negro Progress," *Emporia Gazette* (KS), September 16, 1925, 2.

42. JES to Du Bois, February 9, 1925, in Aptheker, *Correspondence*, 1:304.

43. JES to Hope Spingarn, May 21, 1926, MSRC-JES, Family Correspondence.

44. JES to Hope Spingarn, May 8 and October 31, 1927, January 30, 1928, all in MSRC-JES, Family Correspondence.

45. JES to Hope Spingarn, February 14, 1929, MSRC-JES, Family Correspondence.

46. JES, "Politics and the Poet," 78.

Chapter 10 • Ongoing Challenges and Final Change

1. JES to ABS, April 18, 1930, LOC-ABS, reel 1.

2. Vann to Du Bois, December 26, 1930, and Du Bois to Vann, December 29, 1930, both in Aptheker, *Correspondence*, 1:431–32.

3. JES, "Politics and the Poet," 76–77.

4. JES to ABS, April 19, 1929, LOC-ABS, reel 1; Du Bois, *Dusk of Dawn*, 295.

5. Du Bois, *Dusk of Dawn*, 290–91; JES, "Racial Equality," address delivered May 17, 1932, at the annual conference of the NAACP, Washington, DC, quoted in Van Deusen, *J. E. Spingarn*, 72; JES, "Remarks at the Annual Meeting, January 4, 1931," typescript, LOC-NAACP, box 1.

6. Ross, *J. E. Spingarn*, 134–35.

7. JES to ABS, January 1932, LOC-ABS, reel 1.

8. White to JES, July 11, 1934, LOC-NAACP, box 1; Du Bois to JES, March 27, 1926, BRBML-JES; Ovington quoted in Wedin, *Inheritors*, 253–54.

9. Wilkins, *Standing Fast*, 149.

10. Johnson to Amy Spingarn, August 31, 1932, BRBML-JES.

11. "Reminiscences of Arthur Spingarn," 10, 27–28.

12. JES to Ovington, March 28, 1933, NYPL-JES, box 9.

13. "Stenographic Report of the Address of Mr. J. E. Spingarn before the Twentieth Annual Mass Meeting of the NAACP, 1931," LOC-NAACP, box, 1.

14. "The 23rd Conference," *Crisis* 39 (June 1932): 218.

15. Redding to JES, September 2, 1933, SCMA-WDB, ser. 1.

16. Ross, *J. E. Spingarn*, 184–85; Johnson to Amy Spingarn, September 23, 1933, BRBML-JES.

17. Bates, "New Crowd," 341.

18. Du Bois, *Dusk of Dawn*, 300.

19. Du Bois, "Segregation," 20.

20. JES to Du Bois, March 27, 1934, quoted in Janken, *White*, 189.

21. JES to the Board of Directors, April 5, 1934, LOC-NAACP, box 1.

22. Quoted in Ross, *J. E. Spingarn*, 195–96.

23. Du Bois to ABS, December 15, 1933, MSRC-ABS; JES to ABS, handwritten note, 1934, BRBML-JES.

24. "Preliminary Report of the Committee on Future Plan and Program of the NAACP," LOC-NAACP, box 1.

25. JES, "The Second Quarter Century of the NAACP," address to the annual conference of the NAACP, St. Louis, MO, June 25, 1935, LOC-NAACP, box 1.

26. White, *A Man Called White*, 142–43.

27. "Reminiscences of Arthur Spingarn," 16.

28. Quoted in Taylor, *Zora and Langston*, 184.

29. Hurston to ABS, March 25, 1931, in Kaplan, *Zora Neale Hurston*, 215; Taylor, *Zora and Langston*, 194–209.

30. Meier and Rudwick, "Attorneys Black and White," 937.

31. Sullivan, *Lift Every Voice*, 159.

32. White, *A Man Called White*, 142.

33. Sullivan, *Lift Every Voice*, 230.

34. "Arthur Spingarn Honored," *Chicago Defender*, February 23, 1935.

35. Locke to Houston, June 21, 1935, in Sullivan, *Lift Every Voice*, 208.

36. Sullivan, *Lift Every Voice*, 229–33.

37. "Reminiscences of Arthur Spingarn," 18.

38. Ross, *J. E. Spingarn*, 152–55.

39. "Reminiscences of Arthur Spingarn," 20.

40. Sullivan, *Lift Every Voice*, 196.

41. JES to ABS, November 12, 1937, LOC-ABS, reel 1.

42. Sullivan, *Lift Every Voice*, 229.

43. JES, "Clematis for the Northeastern States," *Bulletin of Popular Information of the Arnold Arboretum* 5, no. 8 (July 1937): 41.

44. JES, *Clematis at Troutbeck* (June 1933), and Stephen Fairbanks to Amy Spingarn, October 15, 1950, both at NYBG-JES; Mumford, Introduction, 74.

45. "Oral History Interview with Stephen J. Spingarn."

46. Virginia A. Buechele, "J. E. Spingarn of Troutbeck, Amenia, NY," typescript prepared for Friends of the Poughkeepsie Rural Cemetery, October 19, 2008, www. poughkeepsieruralcemetery.com.

47. Du Bois, *Dusk of Dawn*, 255.

Chapter 11 • *A New Era for Old Soldiers*

1. "Arthur Spingarn Elected NAACP President," *Crisis* 47, no. 2 (February 19, 1940): 53.

2. "Reminiscences of Arthur Spingarn," 9.

3. Greenberg, *Crusaders in the Courts*, 20.

4. *New York Age*, September 27, 1941.

5. Sullivan, *Lift Every Voice*, 267.

6. Ovington, *Walls*, 174.

7. Ovington, *Walls*, 173.

8. Sullivan, *Lift Every Voice*, 272.

9. ABS, "If I Were a Negro," 2.

10. John H. Johnson to ABS, April 6, 1943, LOC-ABS, reel 1.

11. ABS, "The Jew as a Racial Minority," 2.

12. ABS, "Commencement Address," *Talladegan*, November 1940, 2.

13. W. G. Rogers, "Four Centuries of Negro Books in Largest Private Collection," Associated Press, n.d., copy in MSRC-ABS, Reviews and Notices.

14. ABS, "Collecting a Library," 12.

15. Remarks upon award of Spingarn Medal to Langston Hughes, June 28, 1960, copy in MSRC-ABS, Addresses and Writings.

16. Thompson, "Arthur Barnett Spingarn," 64.

17. Bernhard Knollenberg to ABS, January 20, 1942, James Weldon Johnson Memorial Collection, Beinecke Rare Book and Manuscript Library, Yale University, New Haven, CT.

18. "Howard Acquires Book Collection," *New York Times*, May 30, 1948.

19. Julious Hill to ABS, June 26, 1937, Leon Harris to ABS, March 19, 1949, and J. M. Harrison to ABS, n.d., all in MSRC-ABS, Correspondence.

20. Thompson, "Arthur Barnett Spingarn," 65.

21. Martin, "From Slavery to Freedom," 403.

22. Amy Spingarn to ABS, November 1, 1943, LOC-ABS, reel 1.

23. Arthur Collins to Amy Spingarn, June 24, 1953, NYBG-JES.

24. Brooks to ABS, September 2, 1943, August 20, 1944, January 24, 1945, June 10, 1947, all in LOC-ABS, reel 1.

25. Sullivan, *Lift Every Voice*, 287–88.

26. Quoted in Janken, *White*, 292.

27. Quoted in "Our Loss," *Crisis* 54, no. 6 (May 1945): 141.

28. Sullivan, *Lift Every Voice*, 353.

29. "Reminiscences of Arthur Spingarn," 21.

30. Quoted in Lewis, *W. E. B. Du Bois*, 645.

31. ABS to Alice Crawford, December 19, 1951, SCMA-WDB; typescript for speech, n.d., MSRC-ABS, Addresses and Writings.

32. Greenberg, *Crusaders in the Courts*, 199.

33. "NAACP Sets Advanced Goals," *New York Times*, May 18, 1954, 16.

34. Quoted in "Conference Notes," *Crisis* 61, no. 7 (August–September 1954): 428–29.

35. Sullivan, *Lift Every Voice*, 423.

36. James Ivy, "Arthur Spingarn, Different Man to Different People," *Pittsburgh Courier*, May 12, 1956.

37. "Reminiscences of Arthur Spingarn," 28.

38. Farnsworth Fowles, "Arthur Spingarn of NAACP Is Dead," *New York Times*, December 2, 1971.

39. Eugene Spagnoli, "NAACP Head Hits on March on Capital," *New York Daily News*, July 3, 1963.

40. Both quotes in Thompson, "Arthur Barnett Spingarn," 63.

41. Gary, "White Warrior," 64–65.

42. "Reminiscences of Arthur Spingarn," 18–19, 22–24.

43. James W. Ivy, "Arthur B. Spingarn, Retiring NAACP President," and "Arthur Spingarn: Humanist and Bookman," *Crisis* 73, no. 2 (February 1966): 75–77.

44. "Reminiscences of Arthur Spingarn," 18.

45. "Spingarn's Work Hailed at Rites," *New York Times*, December 6, 1971.

Epilogue • Beyond Brotherhood

1. "President Spingarn Dies," *Crisis* 46, no. 9 (September 1939): 268.

2. Lewis, *W. E. B. Du Bois*, 485, 490.

3. "President Spingarn Dies," 269.

4. JES, autobiographical notes, NYPL-JES.

5. Sorin, *Tradition Transformed*, 6.

6. Quoted in Diner, *In the Almost Promised Land*, 71.

7. Quoted in Thompson, "Arthur Barnett Spingarn," 54.

8. Ross, *J. E. Spingarn*, 13.

9. Abby Ellis, "The Hotel Historian Is at Your Service," *New York Times*, August 7, 2019.

10. Mike Stanton, "Student Financial Aid Boosted by Gift," *Columbia Spectator* (January 20, 1993): 1.

11. Janken, *White*, 369–70.

Addams, Jane. "The Progressive Party and the Negro." *Crisis* 5, no. 1 (November 1912): 30–31.

Anbinder, Tyler. *City of Dreams*. New York: Houghton Mifflin Harcourt, 2016.

Aptheker, Herbert, ed. *The Correspondence of W. E. B. Du Bois*, vol. 1: *1877–1934*. Amherst: University of Massachusetts Press, 1973.

Baker, Ray S., ed. *Woodrow Wilson: Life and Letters*, vol. 4: *1913–1914*. Garden City, NY: Doubleday, 1931.

Barnett, Randy E., and Josh Blackman. *Constitutional Law: Cases in Context*. 2nd ed. New York: Wolters Kluwer, 2017.

Bates, Beth Tompkins. "A New Crowd Challenges the Agenda of the Old Guard in the NAACP, 1933–1941." *American Historical Review* 102, no. 2 (April 1997): 340–77.

Bender, Eugene I. "Reflections on Negro-Jewish Relationships: The Historical Dimension." *Phylon* 30 (Spring 1969): 56–65.

Benton, Charles. *Troutbeck: A Dutchess County Homestead*. Poughkeepsie, NY: Dutchess County Historical Society, 1916.

Broderick, Francis L. *Progressivism at Risk: Electing a President in 1912*. New York: Greenwood, 1989.

Brooks, Van Wyck. *Days of the Phoenix: The Nineteen-Twenties I Remember*. New York: Dutton, 1957.

Broussard, Albert S. *African-American Odyssey: The Stewarts, 1853–1963*. Lawrence: University Press of Kansas, 1998.

Cane, Melville. *All and Sundry: An Oblique Autobiography*. New York: Harcourt, Brace, 1937.

Carle, Susan D. "Race, Class, and Legal Ethics in the Early NAACP (1910–1920)." *Law and History Review* 20, no. 1 (Spring 2002): 97–146.

Chace, James. *1912*. New York: Simon and Schuster, 2004.

Chaddock, Katherine E. *The Multi-Talented Mr. Erskine: Shaping Mass Culture through Great Books and Fine Music*. New York: Palgrave Macmillan, 2012.

Clements, Amy Root. *The Art of Prestige: The Formative Years of Knopf, 1915–1929*. Amherst: University of Massachusetts Press, 2014.

C. M. N. "The New Hesperides by Joel Spingarn." *Sewanee Review* 19, no. 4 (October 1911): 508–9.

Cooper, John Milton, Jr. *Reconsidering Woodrow Wilson: Progressivism, Internationalism, War, and Peace*. Baltimore, MD: Johns Hopkins University Press, 2008.

Dalin, David G. *Jewish Justices of the Supreme Court: From Brandeis to Kagan*. Waltham, MA: Brandeis University Press, 1917.

Diner, Hasia R. *In the Almost Promised Land: American Jews and Blacks, 1915–1935*. Baltimore, MD: Johns Hopkins University Press, 1995.

Du Bois, W. E. B. *The Amenia Conference: An Historic Negro Gathering*. Amenia, NY: Privately printed at Troutbeck Press, 1925.

——. "The American Jew." *Crisis* 4, no. 5 (August 1922): 152.

——. *The Autobiography of W. E. B. Du Bois*. New York: International Publishers, 1968.

——. "Brandeis." *Crisis* 11, no. 5 (March 1916): 243.

——. "Close Ranks." *Crisis* 16, no. 3 (July 1918): 93.

——. *Dusk of Dawn*. New York: Harcourt, Brace and World, 1940.

——. "Editorial: A Momentous Proposal." *Crisis* 16, no. 5 (September 1918): 215–16.

——. "Fighting Race Calumny." *Crisis* 10, no. 1 (May 1915): 40–42.

——. *The Gift of Black Folk: The Negroes in the Making of America*. New York: Washington Square Press, 1970.

——. "Legal Work." *Crisis* 9, no. 6 (April 1915): 289.

——. "Of the Training of Black Men." *Atlantic Monthly* 90 (September 1902): 289–97.

——. "The Perpetual Dilemma." *Crisis* 13, no. 6 (April 1917): 170–71.

——. "The Relation of the Negroes to the Whites in the South." *Annals of the American Academy of Political and Social Science* 18 (July 1901): 121–40.

——. "Returning Soldiers." *Crisis* 18, no. 1 (May 1919): 14.

——. "Segregation." *Crisis* 41, no. 4 (January 1934): 20.

——. *The Souls of Black Folk*. Chicago, IL: McClurg, 1903.

——. "Steve Greene's Story." *Crisis* 1, no. 1 (November 1910): 14.

——. "The Strivings of the Negro People." *Atlantic Monthly* 79 (August 1897): 134–42.

Ellis, Mark. "W. E. B. Du Bois and the Formation of Black Opinion in World War I: A Commentary on 'the Damnable Dilemma.'" *Journal of American History* 81, no. 4 (March 1995): 1584–90.

Erskine, John. *The Memory of Certain Persons: An Autobiography*. New York: Lippincott, 1947.

——. *My Life as a Teacher*. New York: Lippincott, 1948.

Finch, Minnie. *The NAACP: Its Fight for Justice*. Metuchen, NJ: Scarecrow Press, 1981.

Gary, Beverly. "White Warrior." *Negro Digest* (September 1962): 62–67.

Giddings, Paula. "Missing in Action: Ida B. Wells, the NAACP, and the Historical Record." *Meridians* 1, no. 7 (Spring 2001): 1–17.

Ginn, Richard Van Ness. *The History of the U.S. Army Medical Service Corps*. Washington, DC: Office of the Surgeon General, 1997.

Greenberg, Jack. *Crusaders in the Courts: How a Dedicated Band of Lawyers Fought for the Civil Rights Revolution*. New York: Basic, 1994.

Harrison-Kahan, Lori. "Scholars and Knights: W. E. B. Du Bois and J. E. Spingarn, and the NAACP." *Jewish Social Studies: History, Culture, Society* 18, no. 1 (Fall 2011): 63–87.

Hastie, William H. "Toward an Egalitarian Legal Order, 1930–1950." *Annals of the American Academy of Political and Social Science* 407, no. 1 (May 1973): 18–31.

Hofstadter, Richard. *Anti-Intellectualism in American Life*. New York: Knopf, 1963.

Hoopes, James. *Van Wyck Brooks: In Search of American Culture*. Amherst: University of Massachusetts Press, 1977.

Hovey, R. B. "George Edward Woodberry: Gentile Exile." *New England Quarterly* 23, no. 4 (December 1950): 504–26.

Hughes, Langston. *Fight for Freedom: The Story of the NAACP*. New York: Norton, 1962.

Janken, Kenneth Robert. *White: The Biography of Walter White, Mr. NAACP*. New York: New Press, 2003.

Johnson, James Weldon. *Along This Way: The Autobiography of James Weldon Johnson*. New York: Viking, 1933.

Jordan, William. "The Damnable Dilemma: African-American Accommodation and Protest during World War I." *Journal of American History* 81, no. 4 (March 1995): 1562–83.

Kaplan, Carla, ed. *Zora Neale Hurston: A Life in Letters*. Garden City, NY: Doubleday, 2002.

Kellogg, Charles Flint. *NAACP: A History of the National Association of Colored People*. Baltimore, MD: Johns Hopkins University Press, 1967.

Kennedy, David M. *Over Here: The First World War and American Society*. New York: Oxford University Press, 1980.

Keppel, Frederick P. *Columbia*. New York: Oxford University Press, 1914.

Klingenstein, Susanne. *Jews in the American Academy, 1900–1940: The Dynamics of Intellectual Assimilation*. New Haven, CT: Yale University Press, 1991.

Knopf, Alfred A. "The Columbia I Remember." In *University on the Heights*, ed. Wesley First, 179–96. Garden City, NY: Doubleday, 1969.

Lewis, David Levering. "Parallels and Divergences: Assimilationist Strategies of Afro-American and Jewish Elites from 1910 to the Early 1930s." *Journal of American History* 71, no. 3 (December 1984): 543–64.

——. *W. E. B. Du Bois: Biography of a Race*. New York: Henry Holt, 1993.

Lewis, Thomas S. W. "Mumford and the Academy." *Salmagundi*, no. 49 (Summer 1980): 99–111.

Lewisohn, Ludwig. *Upstream: An American Chronicle*. New York: Horace Liveright, 1922.

Logan, Rayford W., ed. *W. E. B. Du Bois: A Profile*. New York: Hill and Wang, 1971.

Martin, Tony. "From Slavery to Freedom, Third Edition: Snapshot from the Life of a Book." *Journal of Negro History* 75, no. 3 (Summer 2009): 402–6.

McCaughey, Robert A. *Stand, Columbia: A History of Columbia University in the City of New York*. New York: Columbia University Press, 2003.

Meier, August. *Negro Thought in America, 1880–1915: Racial Ideologies in the Age of Booker T. Washington*. Ann Arbor: University of Michigan Press, 1963.

Meier, August, and Elliott Rudwick, eds. *Along the Color Line: Explorations in the Black Experience*. Urbana: University of Illinois Press, 1976.

——. "Attorneys Black and White: A Case Study of Race Relations within the NAACP." *Journal of American History* 64, no. 4 (March 1976): 913–46.

Melnick, Ralph. *The Life and Work of Ludwig Lewisohn*, vol. 1: *A Touch of Wildness*. Detroit, MI: Wayne State University Press, 1998.

Morison, Elting E., ed. *The Letters of Theodore Roosevelt*. Vol. 7. Cambridge, MA: Harvard University Press, 1951.

Morris, Edmund. *Theodore Rex.* New York: Modern Library, 2001.

Mowry, George E. "The South and the Progressive Lily White Party of 1912." *Journal of Southern History* 6, no. 2 (May 1940): 237–47.

Mumford, Lewis. Introduction to "Politics and the Poet: A Prophecy." *Atlantic* 170 (November 1942): 73–74.

———. "Scholar and Gentleman." *Saturday Review of Literature* 20 (August 5, 1939): 8–9.

Mutzenberg, Charles G. *Kentucky's Famous Feuds and Tragedies.* New York: R. F. Fenno, 1917.

"Oral History Interview with Stephen J. Spingarn." Interview with Jerry N. Hess, March 20, 1967. Harry S. Truman Library, Independence, MO.

Ovington, Mary White. *Black and White Sat Down Together: The Reminiscences of an NAACP Founder.* New York: Feminist Press, 1995.

———. *Half a Man: The Status of the Negro in New York.* London: Longmans, Green, 1911.

———. "The National Association for the Advancement of Colored People." *Journal of Negro History* 9, no. 2 (April 1924): 107–16.

———. *The Walls Came Tumbling Down.* New York: Harcourt, Brace, 1947.

President's Committee on Civil Rights. *To Secure These Rights: The Report of the President's Committee on Civil Rights.* Washington, DC: N.p., 1947.

Randall, John Herman, Jr., ed. *A History of the Faculty of Philosophy, Columbia University.* New York: Columbia University Press, 1957.

"The Reminiscences of Arthur Spingarn." Interview with Thomas Hogan, July 7, 1966. Typescript, Columbia University Oral History Research Office, New York.

Rosenthal, Michael. *Nicholas Miraculous: The Amazing Career of the Redoubtable Dr. Nicholas Murray Butler.* New York: Farrar, Straus and Giroux, 2006.

Ross, B. Joyce. *J. E. Spingarn and the Rise of the NAACP, 1911–1939.* New York: Atheneum, 1972.

Rudwick, Elliott M. "The Niagara Movement." *Journal of Negro History* 43, no. 1 (July 1957): 177–97.

Sacks, Marcy S. *Before Harlem: The Black Experience in New York City before World War I.* Philadelphia: University of Pennsylvania Press, 2006.

Salzman, Jack, and Cornel West, eds. *Struggles in the Promised Land: Toward a History of Black-Jewish Relations in the United States.* New York: Oxford University Press, 1997.

Sanders, Ronald. *The Downtown Jews: Portrait of an Immigrant Generation.* New York: Harper and Row, 1969.

Santayana, George. "Genteel Tradition in American Philosophy." In *The Genteel Tradition: Nine Essays*, ed. Douglas Wilson, 107–28. Cambridge, MA: Harvard University Press, 1967.

Seligman, Isaac N. "David L. Einstein." *Publications of the American Jewish Historical Society*, no. 19 (1910): 193–96.

Sevitch, Benjamin. "W. E. B. Du Bois and Jews: A Lifetime of Opposing Anti-Semitism." *Journal of African American History* 87 (Summer 2002): 323–37.

Sinclair, Upton. *The Goose-Step: A Study of American Education.* Pasadena, CA: Published by the author, 1922.

Sorin, Gerald. *Tradition Transformed: The Jewish Experience in America.* Baltimore, MD: Johns Hopkins University Press, 1997.

Spingarn, Amy Einstein. *Humility and Pride.* New York: Harcourt, Brace, 1926.

Spingarn, Arthur B. "Collecting a Library of Negro Literature." *Journal of Negro Education* 7, no. 1 (January 1938): 12–18.

———. "If I Were a Negro." Unpublished typescript, 1943. Arthur B. Spingarn Papers, Moorland-Spingarn Research Center, Howard University, Washington, DC.

———. "The Jew as a Racial Minority." Unpublished typescript, n.d. Addresses and Writings, Moorland-Spingarn Research Center, Howard University, Washington, DC.

———. *Laws Relating to Sex Morality in New York City.* New York: Century, 1915.

———. "The War and Venereal Disease among Negroes." *Social Hygiene* 4, no. 3 (July 1918): 23–31.

Spingarn, Joel E. *Creative Criticism: Essays on the Unity of Genius and Taste.* New York: Henry Holt, 1917.

———, ed. *Criticism in America: Its Function and Status.* New York: Harcourt, Brace, 1924.

———. "George Edward Woodberry." In *Dictionary of American Biography*, 10:479–81. New York: Charles Scribner's Sons, 1937.

———. "Henry Winthrop Sargent and the Landscape Tradition at Wodenethe." *Landscape Architecture Magazine* 29, no. 1 (October 1938): 24–39.

———. "Lyly's 'Endimion.'" *Athenaeum*, no. 3484 (August 4, 1894): 172.

———. *The New Criticism.* New York: Columbia University Press, 1911.

———. *The New Hesperides and Other Poems.* New York: Sturgis and Walton, 1911.

———. "The Origins of Modern Criticism." *Modern Philology* 1, no. 4 (April 1904): 477–96.

———. *Poems.* New York: Harcourt, Brace, 1924.

———. "Politics and the Poet: A Prophecy." *Atlantic Monthly* 170 (November 1942): 75–78.

———. "Prothalamion." *Atlantic Monthly* 89 (April 1902): 518–20.

———. *A Question of Academic Freedom: Being the Official Correspondence between Nicholas Murray Butler, President of Columbia University, and J. E. Spingarn, Professor of Comparative Literature in Columbia University, during the Academic Year 1910–1911.* New York: Printed for distribution among the alumni, 1911.

———. *A Scholar's Testament.* Amenia, NY: Troutbeck Press, 1931.

———. "The Younger Generation: A New Manifesto." *Freeman* 5 (June 1922): 296–98.

Sullivan, Patricia. *Lift Every Voice: The NAACP and the Making of the Civil Rights Movement.* New York: New Press, 2009.

Taylor, Yuval. *Zora and Langston.* New York: Norton, 2019.

Thirty Years of Lynching in the United States, 1889–1918. New York: NAACP, 1919.

Thompson, Francis H. "Arthur Barnett Spingarn: Advocate for Black Rights." *Historian* 50, no. 1 (November 1987): 54–66.

Tuttle, William M., Jr. "W. E. B. Du Bois' Confrontation with White Liberalism during the Progressive Era." *Phylon* 35, no. 3 (1974): 241–58.

Van Deusen, Marshall. *J. E. Spingarn.* New York: Twayne, 1971.

Villard, Oswald Garrison. *Fighting Years: Memoirs of a Liberal Editor.* New York: Harcourt, Brace, 1939.

Vitelli, James R. *Van Wyck Brooks.* New York: Twayne, 1969.

Washington, Joseph R., Jr., ed. *Jews in Black Perspectives: A Dialogue.* Teaneck, NJ: Fairleigh Dickinson University Press, 1984.

Wedin, Carolyn. *Inheritors of the Spirit: Mary White Ovington and the Founding of the NAACP.* New York: Wiley, 1998.

Weinberg, Meyer, ed. *The World of W. E. B. Du Bois: A Quotation Sourcebook.* Westport, CT: Greenwood, 1992.

White, Walter. *A Man Called White: The Autobiography of Walter White.* New York: Viking, 1948.

———. *Rope and Faggot: A Biography of Judge Lynch.* New York: Knopf, 1929.

Wilkins, Roy. *Standing Fast: The Autobiography of Roy Wilkins.* New York: Viking, 1982.

Woodson, Carter. *The Negro Professional Man and the Community, with Special Emphasis on the Physician and the Lawyer.* Washington, DC: Association for the Study of Negro Life and History, 1934.

Wright, George C. "The NAACP and Residential Segregation in Louisville, Kentucky, 1914–1917." *Register of the Kentucky Historical Society* 78, no. 1 (Winter 1980): 39–54.

ALSO BY
KATHERINE REYNOLDS CHADDOCK

Uncompromising Activist

Richard Greener, First Black Graduate of Harvard College

Katherine Reynolds Chaddock

Almost forgotten until his papers were discovered in a Chicago attic, Richard Greener was a pioneer who broke educational and professional barriers for Black citizens.

The Johns Hopkins University Studies in Historical and Political Science Series

press.jhu.edu

CPSIA information can be obtained
at www.ICGtesting.com
Printed in the USA
BVHW031946040123
655567BV00006B/13/J

9 781421 445519